From the Bestselling Author of *How to Succeed Against All Odds!*

NETWORK MARKETING

How to Avoid the Damage It Can Do to Your Life and Business and

How to SUCCEED!

(Is Network Marketing Good for You & Your Business?)

By

MARGARET DUREKE, JD

"One of the most valuable trainers for Blacks in Government."
— Blacks In Government 2010 NTC Chair, Jacque Ballard

"One of the Nation's TOP Network Marketing Gurus!"
— Bernard McCargo, Network Marketing Legend

Printed and produced in the United States of America.

Library of Congress Control Number: 2010909700

JAHS ISBN: 978-0-9747550-3-8

FIRST EDITION

Senior Editor:	Lynn Burns (The WordPlace)
Cover Artwork:	Chi-Chi Dureke
Cover Design:	Chi-Chi Dureke and Wally Burns
Copy Editing:	John Dureke, Lynn and Wally Burns
Technical Layout:	Margaret Dureke, Chi-Chi Dureke, Wally Burns
Typesetting:	Margaret Dureke, Wally Burns

JAHS Publishing Group

Publisher of *FACES OF POWER* magazine
Margaretspeaks.com
"Read and Be Inspired"

Mailing Address:

P.O. Box 1164
Riverdale, Maryland 20738
Telephone: 301-864-2800
E-mail: info@jahspublishing.com

Order Online:

www.jahspublishing.com
www.margaretspeaks.com
www.margaretssisterslivingonpurpose.com
www.successmarketingstrategies101.com

JAHS Family Sites:

www.JAHStelecom.com
www.womenempoweredtoachievetheimpossible.com
www.teamunited4-3.com
www.jahsfitness.com
www.jahsactivewear.com
www.chichisart.com

I would like to dedicate this book to Wally and Lynn Burns for believing in me unconditionally.

About Margaret Dureke, JD

Margaret Dureke has a BA from Howard University and a Juris Doctorate Degree in Law from American University. She is a national and international entrepreneur extraordinaire, Publisher, Best Selling Author, Renowned "Moxie Motivational" and Inspirational Speaker, Personal and Business Success Coach, Leadership Trainer, Radio and TV personality. Margaret is a happily married mother of three beautiful children. Some of Margaret's online success platforms: www.margaretspeaks.com; www.margaretssisterlivingonpurpose.com; www.womenempoweredtoachievetheimpossible.com; www.Successmarketingstrategies101.com.

Margaret Dureke and her husband John Dureke have founded and run many successful traditional businesses, amongst which are: www.jahspublishing.com; www.jahsfitness.com; www.jahsactivewear.com.

However, over time, *they realized that they could not build wealth sitting in one place from 9-5*, and they *could not build wealth in isolation.* They realized that true financial freedom will only come through leveraging the efforts of others, diversification of earnings, and creating a duplicate-able system that leads to an extraordinary income and lifestyle that comes from ordinary effort. So, Margaret and her husband John Dureke joined their first telecom network marketing company 5 years ago and became Senior Vice Presidents with that company and Triple Diamonds with another company in record time before finding their home with PHPI; they are also part of the Founding Members of People Helping People, Inc. (PHPI). Margaret has been quoted in *The Washington Post* for defending the network industry.

Some of Margaret's past and present Clients:
America Online (AOL) • BET.com • SAM'S Club • Merck & Company • DOT • U.S. Dept. of the Treasury • U.S. Coast Guard • National Defense University • FBI • Maryland Dept. of Mental

Hygiene, Alcohol and Drug Abuse • National Progressive Baptist Convention • Washington Hospital Center • Howard University • University of Maryland • Blacks In Government. Ms. Dureke's success stories have been featured in many publications, including: *The Washington Post* • BET.Com • *Heart & Soul* magazine • *Sister 2 Sister* magazine.

What **American University** said after Margaret's success story was published in *The Washington Post*: *"On behalf of the faculty, staff and students, I congratulate and commend you on your success with your business ventures…these are outstanding achievements and a great source of pride to our school."* – Mary Catherine Somerset, Director of Alumni Relations, Washington College of Law, the American University

Purpose of the Book

Have you fallen victim to the PROMISED next best thing since Microsoft and spent your entire fortune on it hoping to make endless amounts of cash with it month after month? Have you given up your dream of making it big with a network marketing business? Do you think it is a scam like most people think and drawn a foregone conclusion? Did you get burnt by "one of those pyramid things" – the first one you tried and swore that you will never touch one again with the longest spoon in the world?

Did it work out, or were you left high and dry with barely two nickels to rub together? Have you also gotten too deep with the first or second or even third MLM company you got involved with to the point of no return or so you think?

This book has answers as to how you can flush out your loss and restore your financial well-being. Or have you always been interested but afraid to get involved because of the fear of the unknown?

~In life and business, you don't get what you want or deserve, but what you <u>negotiate</u> and <u>make happen</u>!~

Have you lost all your family members, friends, and co-workers, church members, messed up your relationships with people who trusted you because you brought them into your network business? Are you looking to see if network marketing could be the avenue to use to earn a living or diversify your income, but you're not sure? Have you been in a network marketing business for some time now but just can't seem to quit and don't know why you have not yet gotten it right to make the kind of money you know you could make? Are you running a traditional business, but you're struggling or not successful and need a new insight? This book is also for you.

If you answered 'yes' even remotely to any of these questions, this book is for you. **I invite you to read this book thoughtfully and intently and learn how to stop making the common mistakes many make every day in network marketing businesses and start earning REAL MONEY because there is a lot of money in this TRILLION DOLLAR industry.** Learn how!!!!!!!!!

I believe that it is not the industry per se that is the problem or the reason why you did not make it. It is not necessarily the products and services associated with the industry that are the culprit. I will admit though that there are some ills with the industry which I have addressed herewith. However, by the time you digest and dissect this book in its entirety, you will see the mistakes you made, learn the ways to get involved and make what you want out of it. And if you are already involved and may be at the point of no return and basically stuck, you will learn how to un-stuck yourself, regroup, re-structure, re-strategize and **flush out** your losses and profit. This industry has set a lot of families financially free and opened doors to other opportunities for many people who would never have been able to get into them without first getting involved with MLM.

Then there are those who think that network marketing is for those people who don't have money or a "good job". I guess the current devastating recession has proven to us that everyone needs to have plans "A" and "B" and in some instances multiple plans – as proven by Donald Trump and my father-in-law J. C. M. Dureke and his father who had the foresight in their time to understand and build multiple streams of income by owning multiple businesses that yielded multiple streams of income.

What I say to those with the illusion that they don't need network marketing because they have a good job or are educated, is that if you know how much you have in the bank, you are not rich/wealthy. You are allowing someone else to determine your worth. Also, remember that if any employer pays you $50.00 per hour, he or she must be making 3-5 times of your effort. Let's face it; no one will pay you for a loss. Wealthy and rich people don't know exactly how much they have in the bank. They simply know approximately how much they are worth and not the exact amount they have in the bank. Put another way, if someone else determines how much you make or what you are worth, you are still in bondage because you will never grow beyond the

confinement in which you find yourself –
consciously or unconsciously!

The problem is that so many people are busy being
skeptical instead of keeping an open mind that could
be the difference between finding 'the one' and
living in denial all their lives – protecting the life
they don't want in the first place instead of pushing
the envelope beyond normalcy to see if this could be
'the one' and fight for the life they want and have
always dreamed of!

Table of Contents

The Damage Network Marketing Can Do to Your Life and Business and How to Restore Them

~In life and business, you don't get what you want or deserve, but what you <u>negotiate</u> and <u>make happen</u>!~

How to Avoid the Damage Network Marketing Can Do to Your Life and Business

~In life and business, you don't get what you want or deserve, but what you <u>negotiate</u> and <u>make happen</u>!~

How to Succeed in Network Marketing

~In life and business, you don't get what you want or deserve, but what you <u>negotiate</u> and <u>make happen</u>!~

Foreword by Betty Miles

Dear Margaret, I am honored to be a part of promoting your book because I think there is a tremendous need for honesty and transparency when reviewing and analyzing the pros and cons of network marketing! There is a difficult struggle ahead of us if we are to gain the credibility we desire!! We must take the high road of integrity rather than the low one of expediency. You are one of the few pure spirits I've met who could make this happen, and I would so love to see that happen!!

This is an incredible book written by one of the most dynamic and successful people I have ever met!! She has addressed all the questions that have plagued many of us who love network marketing, but dislike the reputation a few dishonest and unscrupulous individuals have given it!! If you will follow Margaret Dureke's advice, you will find that this industry can make all of your financial dreams a probability rather than a possibility!!

*— **Betty Miles**, a lawyer, author, "Queen of Network Marketing" and wife of the former Secretary of State of South Carolina*

"Good things come to those who wait but only what is left behind by those who hustled!"

~ Abraham Lincoln

Margaret Dureke's Business Experiences and Background
(from the eyes of one of her clients)

A true testament of anybody's work is best evaluated from the eyes of those they serve.

Hence this story is shared by one of my clients and followers – Ms. Shawnta Ball, a graduate student from the University of Maryland. Ms. Ball interviewed me for one of her class assignments where students were required to interview an entrepreneur of their choice. Ms. Ball decided to interview me after attending one of my workshops and my sessions with the National Blacks In Government Annual Conference. Below is what Shawnta has to write about Margaret Dureke and her husband in the area of successes they have attained in business.

Writing Assignment by Ms. Shawnta Ball

Interview with a Business Owner – Margaret Dureke

Firstly, I'd like to say that as an aspiring entrepreneur, I really enjoyed chapter six on Entrepreneurship and Starting a Small Business. I learned a lot of dos and don'ts, and some of the reasons why businesses fail and how to make them succeed. This chapter has helped me to ask myself some real thought-provoking questions. However, I must say that I was honest with myself and I know that if I can be dedicated and committed to my government job, then I know I can trust myself to make my own business thrive on that same energy, tenacity and more. I know that I already posses many qualities and characteristics in my daily duties at work that will pay off when I own my own business.

Secondly, I am glad I had the opportunity to interview not just any entrepreneur, but one who I can identify with and one who has already accomplished a number of the things I am yet tapping into. I just met Entrepreneur, Margaret Dureke this past August at the Blacks In Government Conference where I had the opportunity to hear her speak on several topics. Then just this past weekend, I attended a workshop where Mrs. ... [She] gave a workshop to encourage and empower women to be enriched and victorious in every area of their lives and to live and strive to live out their dreams on a daily basis.

Mrs. Dureke and her husband Mr. John Dureke are partners in their thriving businesses in which they have several products and services they offer locally, nationally and internationally. The purpose of their business is to make people's lives better and to help them reach heights unknown. However, according to Margaret, they have a parent company that has several subsidiaries and therefore, the form of business is a corporation. To name a few, some of those subsidiaries are: Fitness, Publishing and Authoring (books, magazines, inspirational material,

tools of empowerment, videos, DVDs and CDs),
Motivational Speaking, Providing Conferences,
Workshops, Coaching, and Mentoring.

During my interview with co-owner and co-founder
of JAH's Publishing Company, I saw a direct
correlation in some of the actions and activities
concerning their businesses and some of the
concepts given in chapter six. For instance, pages
162 and 163 talked about causes and failures of
small businesses, which businesses are hard to get
started and hard to keep afloat, versus the
businesses that are easy to start up. However, some
businesses succumb to easy failure as well. As you
continue to read, you will see how the Dureke's have
multiple businesses under one umbrella. I think it
was wise of them to focus on all of their money
making talents, skills, and abilities and not focus
only on their publishing company. Figure 6.4 on
page 162 also talks about people mistaking the
freedom of being in business for oneself for the
liberty to work or not, according to whim. The
Dureke's consistently demonstrate that their

businesses are worth having and the discipline pays off. They don't mind suffering a few afflictions and giving up a few hours of pleasure to reap the profits of multiple healthy businesses and a harvest of wealth.

The Dureke's use the Internet to conduct at least 90% of their business and have learned a lot from their ups/downs and various setbacks. They have been in business for themselves for over 10 years and decided a very long time ago that they wanted more than just a regular 9-5 job. They realized that one can never build wealth sitting in one place for the better part of the day working for someone else. Margaret said that one will never have a chance to do what they are really passionate about if they continue to go about life in this manner. In her speeches, she often uses the quote from the well known Professor, Albert Einstein, "The definition of insanity is doing the same thing over and over again and expecting different results. "

It is no surprise the Dureke's want more out of life and especially for their children. They have instilled the same values, if not more into their children, and at least one of their children who is not even 20 years old yet has her own business and sells art on line. Might I add, the art is her very own drawings and paintings that come from her very own imagination! They are teaching their children early the advantages of being an entrepreneur. According to Margaret the advantages of being in business for yourself is, you are your own boss and in control of your own destiny. She says that it gives her the power to build and create wealth whereas a 9-5 cannot provide such freedom. Another advantage she mentioned, there are no limitations as long as she and her husband continue to stay the course to achieve.

Some of the disadvantages she mentioned are taking a risk and if things don't work out she and her husband really cannot depend on anyone to bail them out. There's also a chance that the corporation may not make any money at times, and that is when *they are reminded of the keys to their success. Their keys to success are resilience, determination, devotion, persistence, prayer, taking the time to invest, sacrifice, and being willing to give up shopping, and other things for the sake of being able to leave a legacy for their children and grand children to come. One of Margaret's mottos is, "To have what you never had you have to be willing to do what you've never done before."*

Margaret says that if she had to do it all over again she would try to get a lump sum of money and then maybe the struggle would not be so hard. It's not that they did not try for loans because they did, but the government never delivered on the promise. On the other hand she takes nothing for granted concerning her journey of where she came from and where she is today. She said to do it all over again would minimize what she has achieved. If she took away the heart of the journey it would change the appreciation and gratitude of what the Lord has done in their lives. She says that the pain helps her to appreciate what has been born out of her spirit.

The good, bad, and ugly, makes it all worth the journey and the person she has become today.

She admits that they came very close many times to shutting down. They ran into issues with landlords and employees who stole money, equipment, products such as books and clothes from their clothing line, but they continued to stay the course instead of succumbing to defeat. Again Figure 6.4 talks about allowing for set back and unexpected expenses on page 162. Obviously, the Dureke's have overcome many obstacles and their businesses are booming!

What I took from the interview as an author myself and aspiring entrepreneur, if you can't take a loss then don't go into business for yourself. Just as the old cliché says, if you can't take the heat, then get out of the kitchen. I know that I will have to sacrifice and give up some things that I am accustomed to, and be willing to take a loss, but yet continue to invest. I read the following statement on the Dureke's Website which explains why they are so inspired to publish books and I quote..., "The publishers understand and value the power of words, particularly in today's world. This is why we are here to bring you books that will not only enrich your life "holistically," but most importantly, books that will help you decipher your calling in life and help you find a meaningful purpose for being here on earth." I value this statement so much because as I said in the beginning, I see so much of myself and the things I want to do in this couple. They are very good models for me and as a result of this interview, I am going to ask Margaret Dureke to be my mentor.

– Shawnta Ball

History of Network Marketing or Direct Sales

Backdrop History of Direct Selling

It has been written and said time without number that the best predictor of something's future is embedded in the past of that matter. As we say in this industry, documentation beats conversation. So is the case here. Let me then give you a little background history of the subject matter at hand from an outside and objective source to help bolster the information I have shared in this book. So, here it is, and it is an excerpt from the Direct Sales Association (DSA):

"The direct seller's activities were influenced, certainly, by the cultures from which they emerged. As early as 2000 B.C., the Code of Hammurabi, a monument of Babylonian law, protected the general welfare and integrity of the Babylonian direct seller, who was then referred to as the 'peddler'. The Code stated that 'the peddler shall swear the oath of God if any enemy caused him trouble in the travels.' It also said that 'the merchant who sells the goods must be aptly compensated.' Trade by land, though hindered by poor roads, continued to grow after the birth of Christ.

In the 5th century A.D., Athens was involved in a great deal of direct selling. Many producers who sold direct to the consumer without the intervention of a middleman, continued to sell their goods in this fashion, despite the growing urban population which spawned a new class of retailers. The direct seller of the 5th century either sold his wares about the street or exhibited them for sale on stalls and in shops. Others traveled from place to place, following armies on the march. They visited great festivals and fairs as well, and sold from village to village.

The 10th century marked the beginning of worldwide economic expansion. As commercial opportunities grew, so did the opportunities for the direct seller. He was the native merchant in Western

Europe, for example, during the Middle Ages, and he played an important role in bringing about the perpetuation of trade during the Commercial Revolution of the 10th to 13th centuries. He witnessed great progress in road building at this time. In France, the direct seller contributed to the growth of trade by bringing 'novelties' from the large cities to small villages. Many of the more prosperous French towns were graced with the opportunity to buy woolen and silk belts, bonnets, brass rings, thimbles and writing tablets from the direct seller.

The traveling merchant was cited in mythology as a notable direct seller. Ulysses, the mythic hero, once posed as a merchant. The little tale, repeated by many ancient authors in many different forms, makes reference to Ulysses as a traveling merchant. He antedates the American peddler by almost 3,000 years. At a palace, Ulysses offered ornaments for sale that he had placed on his arm. The king's daughters were 'engrossed with the contents of the merchant's pack.'

In the 17th century, 'The Winter's Tale' by William Shakespeare, was inspired by a girl peddling flowers. This flower girl was reminiscent of the direct seller of the Middle Ages who walked tirelessly through the village streets displaying his goods.

In early America, for instance, the renowned Yankee Peddler walked to his customers while those of grander stature rode horseback. The prosperous sellers rode in wagons or carriages.

As emigrants began to filter into early American territories in the 18th and 19th centuries, many became **direct sellers**. Like their predecessors, these direct sellers began their treks on trails marked by nature. Good roads developed slowly on the frontiers of early America. Early Indian trails evolved into major roads and eventually turnpikes. As the roadways expanded, the Yankee Peddler's influence on trade was reinforced.

Yankee notions consisted of items like pins, needles, hooks, scissors, combs, small hardware and perfume. The Yankee Peddler carried his goods in oblong tin trunks slung on his back by a harness or a leather strap. Sometimes he used large wagons. He traveled by land primarily until rivers and lakes became connected by canals. Then, direct selling in early America branched out to the frontiers of the West and the Canadian territory in the north. The Yankee Peddlers, as did the Phoenicians, preferred to trade via water routes.

Nearly every culture shares a heritage of direct selling. The direct seller of tropical Africa walked the streets of cities and towns crying out his wares. Some cycled from village to village. 'Colporteurs' of France sold flowers directly to their customers and used purchase orders as early as the 14th century. The Chinese direct seller sold, bought, exchanged, mended, entertained and catered to personal wants of man in almost every conceivable way.

European gypsies, after emigrating to America, practiced their native trade of direct selling in their new land. They brought the direct selling tradition from England, Scotland, Ireland, Germany and

Hungary to Colonial America and took to tinkering, peddling and horse dealing.

The selling tradition continued to thrive through the end of the 19th century and into the 1900s. The advent of the home party in the 1950s added a new dimension to direct selling as customers gathered at the home of hostesses to see product demonstrations and socialize with friends. Direct selling offered opportunities for many who had previously run into barriers because of age, education or sex. The growth of the industry allowed many to become successful where no opportunity had existed before.

Today, at the beginning of the 21st century, the customer still benefits from a personal and convenient way of purchasing products. The Internet has become an important element of direct selling – essentially giving each direct seller a worldwide customer base. Direct sellers have been empowered by use of the Internet and find direct selling to be a rewarding way to improve their quality of life, reach specific earnings objectives, facilitate social contact and sell products they love."

Direct Sales Evolves

Then, let's fast forward to today and you can see how direct selling has evolved to what it is today. And with the present state of the economy, it is about to become the new way in which people will engage to help them secure alternative means of income so that when one source is down, they will have alternatives. I personally believe that the reason why a lot of people fell without warning was because prior to the economic burst, most people lived well with just one source of income. When the economy crumbled, most were caught off guard and were not prepared for what hit them. Most, however, have learned their lesson and have taken to direct sales as a simple, quick and inexpensive way to make a good living.

In fact, because of the economic recession today, direct selling is gaining more ground. More and more people are beginning to pay attention to it, and they are actually willing to take a look at the different opportunities out there that could avail them of the chance to partake in it and profit.

It is not a secret now that Network Marketing (also known as Direct Sales) (also known as face-to-face selling) (also known as Multi-level marketing – MLM) (also known as relationship marketing) ***is a billion dollar industry that many have profited from, and many more are in line to benefit if they know how and are willing to get themselves out of the way.***

So, what is Direct Selling?

Direct selling is the sale of a consumer product or service, person-to-person, away from a fixed retail location, marketed through independent sales representatives who are sometimes also referred to as consultants, distributors or by other titles.

Just about any product or service can be purchased through direct selling somewhere in the world. Many people think of cosmetics, wellness products and home décor as products that are often sold through direct sales, but add to that countless other product categories including kitchen products, jewelry, clothing, organic gardening supplies, spa products, scrapbooking supplies, rubber stamps and much, much more. – *Direct Selling Association (DSA)*

Network Marketing and Direct Sales Stereotypes

If your last experience with direct selling didn't have you in the starring role, perhaps it's time to update your memory bank with an experience in your own living room – or that of the next friend who sends an invite your way. – *Lori Penner, said piece "Why We Love Our Tupperware" that appeared in a Canadian publication and was posted in the DSA blog website of February 19th, 2010.*

The whole idea of the home party was to give the post-war housewife a way to manage her domestic life yet still maintain some of the financial independence she had gained while the boys were busy fighting overseas. She could become a Tupperware consultant and actually earn a dandy little income if her sales were good and she knew how to nag her friends and family.

Other product lines followed, like Mary Kay and Pampered Chef, still using the direct sales approach in someone's crowded living room, with the hostess smiling and serving coffee, hoping sales were good so she could walk away with some free stuff.

The home party gave women a heady sense of freedom, being able to leave the hubby and kids at home for a few hours and purchase some serious timesaving products that no housewife should do without. Being at one of these parties recently made me keenly aware of just how much fun you can have when you throw a bunch of enthusiastic women together. Yet, there was casualness about this get-together I didn't remember from the parties my mother and aunts used to throw.

We did the same oohing and aahing our mothers and their mothers did before them as the consultants proudly displayed their wares. We played the same old ice-breaking games for prizes, nibbled on crackers and cheese, and passed the products from person to person, acting utterly amazed and in awe at the marvels of modern technology, wondering how we could have thought our lives were complete without these things.

It was direct marketing at its best, where you could handle the product; pick the color and style that best suited your individual needs and décor – the same article continued.

No wonder then a lot of people are missing out on the newest and the new "in thing" opportunity to turn anyone's financial well-being around or enhance it. This is because a lot of people are still of the opinion that it is the ladies' pastime and/or just for the ladies to make more income while "the boys" went to the "real job" outside the home. The funny thing is that a good thing can come about from the weakest link or unintended consequence. Meaning that even though the concept of network marketing or direct selling started as Lori Penner's article stipulated, it has now taken a unique and very important and strategic place today in the marketplace. People really need to wake up and realize what time it is now in the marketplace with regards to DSA, in conjunction with internet and social networks. Direct selling is really a remarkable way to earn a living without laboring as much if you know how. The **how** part and to help those who tried before and failed are really the main reasons for this book!

When it comes to Network Marketing a lot of people are very defensive, skeptical, doubtful and egotistical about why it is not for them, when in fact it may be the very best thing that could happen to them. Let's face it, everyone would like to own their own business, be their own boss and to some extent control their own financial destiny. *However, we know that most people can't because of two primary reasons – (a) lack of funding; and (b) lack of expertise, among other factors.*

Betty Miles, the Queen of Network Marketing, Success Story

I recall what Betty Miles, the wife of the former Secretary of State for South Carolina, a good friend of mine, also known as the FIRST Lady of network marketing and business partner of mine told me about what her husband, a noble legal practitioner, said to her when she first told him that she was going to do network marketing.

Betty Miles is a humble woman of honor, integrity and of impeccable character and professionalism with a heart of gold and would go the extra mile and stay the course for what she believes in and for others too.

Margaret Dureke and Betty Miles, a lawyer, the
wife of the former Secretary of State for South
Carolina, the FIRST Lady of Network Marketing,
a woman of honor and integrity who has also
authored many books.

Ms. Betty Miles told me that her husband was
absolutely not going to have it, and he gave her so
many reasons why she should not do multi-level
marketing or direct sales or network marketing.
Amongst those reasons Mr. Miles gave her were:

- Their social status in the community;

- What their friends were going to think about them;
- Mr. Miles' reputation as a lawyer;
- How their friends and associates would see them now;
- Isn't it for people that don't have money?
- Mr. Miles told Betty that Network marketing was for Democrats and not for Republicans – WOW!

However, Betty who is also a lawyer, being the wise and savvy businesswoman that she is, found *creative ways* to convince her husband to let her take part in the business by pointing Mr. Miles to the fact that the network marketing industry is a trillion dollar industry from which many are earning life-changing residual incomes from the comfort of their homes. She further challenged Mr. Miles to use his legal knowledge and expertise to diligently research the industry, and if he found anything to the contrary, she would not become part of the business. Mr. Miles agreed and took Betty up on that challenge. He began to research the DSA industry business and was astounded by what he found. At that point he told his wife Betty to go ahead.

History has it that after she worked her magic to get her husband to see what she saw, being a pioneer and visionary, she went on to make millions in the industry starting with a telecom company called Excel, which a lot of people know made several people millionaires and went on to create generational wealth for those families. Today, Betty is still waxing very strong in the network industry and everyone she knows – especially her family members – are in the business with her because they have seen firsthand what can be achieved with earning residual income just by leveraging one's network and working from home.

For those who are in the network industry and those who now know who she is because of her achievements in network marketing, she has come to be known as the "Queen of Network Marketing."

As we say in this business, *documentation beats conversation any day and any time.* The following is an excerpt from Betty Miles' bestselling book: *The American Dream*, as written by her husband Jim Miles, the former Secretary of State of South Carolina, in his introduction of the book:

When it comes to being "presumed guilty," the only industry with more PR problems than the law or politics would be network marketing. I see it when my wife – a very genuine, talented, competent and successful businesswoman – tells people she's in network marketing. They step back, glance nervously about and start mumbling about "pyramids." To be honest, that was my general impression of the industry, too. I had seen too many chain letters and Ponzi schemes during my days as an attorney to put any credibility in the network marketing concept. So, when Betty first mentioned to me that she was looking at a network marketing business, without even thinking, I said "no."

But Betty, as you will see in the pages following, is no quitter. She kept working on me, challenging my assumptions. She scored points by noting that some people think all lawyers are shysters and all politicians are crooks, but we knew better, didn't we?

Finally, I agreed – unenthusiastically – to check it out. After weeks of research, I concluded that my wife was absolutely right. Like most people, I knew nothing of the contemporary network marketing industry, about changes in their business approach, the large, well-respected businesses that are using network marketing techniques every day. Indeed, my change of heart is so complete that not only have I concluded that network marketing delivers a product or service at a competitive price is legal, but I truly believe it soon will represent the preferred method of delivery of products and services by major companies all over the world.

If you share the negative view of network marketing that I once had, this book is for you. It offers straight answers to your questions about how network marketing really works, about its legal status, its business structure and its compensation systems.

If you understand network marketing, but doubt that it is right for you, then you need this book as well. It tells the stories of people just like you – in their own words – and how they have changed their lives using network marketing to prosper in the new, down-sizing, high-pressure economy. But most of all, this book is for those of you who have begun to doubt yourself, who have given up on the American Dream. Like Betty, I am a dedicated believer in America as the land of opportunity. I am in politics because I want government to be more than a regulator and tax collector. I want government to be my partner – and yours – in achieving the American Dream of economic and personal freedom so you can live your life to the fullest – as decided by you, not someone else. This is America. And in the America of the late 20th century, network marketing offers astounding rewards to those who dare to believe, who dare to dream and dare to achieve. This book will help you believe again by showing you that the dream is still alive. When you finish this book, whether or not you get involved in a single network marketing program, you will know that the bright vision of the future shared by our parents and grandparents is still alive; and, if you look, you might find the vision, too. If you doubt me, then this book is for you.

– Jim Miles, South Carolina Secretary of State, July 4, 1996

Lessons to be Learned from the Betty Miles Success Story

When you get a vision/dream, do not let anyone, not even your loved ones, talk you out of it, even if it does not make sense at the time; even if it is not yet popular.

If you have a vision to start or do something that others may not yet see, have a plan of action on how to succeed: As we all know by now, not everyone is a visionary. You don't have to be blunt about what you want to do if you want your loved ones' support, which I think is very crucial in order to sustain yourself in Multi-Level Marketing (MLM). *Find creative ways*, like Betty did by pointing her husband to a direct source about the opportunity. Again, as we say in this industry, "documentation beats conversation" – especially for lawyers; they are all about documents. So, don't get into a shouting match with your loved ones about why you want to do it, but rather, like Betty, point them to outside, independent sources of credibility toward it.

Take time to explain what it is that you are trying to get into and why it is important to you. If you believe in your cause, no one can stop you. If they do not see it with you, then remind them that the essence of support is not that the person you are seeking support from will understand (in most cases), but rather that they should support you because they love you. You have the right to follow your heart for whatever God has deposited in you – even if it's an unpopular path in the meantime. They should still support you because it will make it easier for you to pursue your goals and ambitions.

In most cases, you will get a reluctant support, but that is okay because if you know what you really want, this reluctance on the part of your loved ones should act as a motivator to make you find creative ways to succeed at your venture. They will be proud of you eventually when you succeed because they now know that you were convicted in your belief.

~In life and business, you don't get what you want or deserve, but what you <u>negotiate</u> and <u>make happen</u>!~

So, I see it as a positive. I honestly would not and could not have become the person that I am today without negative people and circumstances in my life. Negativisms totally motivate me and drive me beyond what most people would be willing to put themselves through to get what they want.

Persistence will break resistance. Think about this for one second. What if Betty had just said the very first time her husband objected to her doing Multi-Level Marketing (MLM), "Okay," and gave up her dreams of making handsome money from the system? No one would know about her today, and no telling whether she would have been as happy as she is today! However, because she was convicted about what she wanted and what she had seen, she persisted and continued to nudge her husband to dare to learn more, and because she persisted, she won eventually.

Persistence produces Perseverance which produces Profit (P4-power). Perseverance is a fruit of the spirit, which often leads to profit because it is only those that persevere that see the grace of God. That is why it baffles me that a lot of people want to get through without going through, and it is not possible. It is like planting no seed and waiting to harvest.

Never quit on your dreams and aspirations, especially if you are greatly convicted of your vision. Never quit on your goals or objectives, but you can quit on the means or channel at hand. Quitters are losers – PERIOD!

In fact, the mental mindset for a whole lot of people about what MLM/DSA can do and should be doing has changed and is changing because many more people are still in the dark about the power of marketing successfully through the network marketing method. It is and has been established that word of mouth is the most powerful means of advertising or marketing, and that is what it is all about. It produces more loyal customers because of the relationship element of it.

Statistical Overview of the Direct Sales and Network Marketing Industry

As I've said before, in the network marketing industry – documentation beats conversation any day, any time. So let's take a look at some hard and independent facts about this industry, where it has been, where it is now and where it is going.

99.9% of the data used here was adopted from the Direct Sales Association (DSA) projections and scientifically gathered data, which is independent of my opinion.

Estimated 2008 U.S. Direct Sales: $29.6 Billion

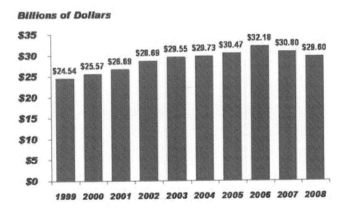

Steadily growing – and one industry that is recession proof is Telecom which is only going one direction – UP!

Estimated 2008 U.S. Salespeople   15.0 Million

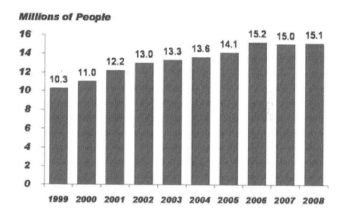

Simply shows that more and more sales people get involved every year. In 1999, the number was 10.3 million and in 2008, 15.1 million. I can bet that by the time the new statistics are published, the numbers will be higher.

Face-to-Face Selling   76.7%

In the home	71.8%
Temporary location	2.5%
Workplace	2.2%
Other Location	0.2%
Remote Selling and Auto shipments	**22.9%**
Internet	11.9%
Phone	8.4%
Other remote selling and auto ship	3.0%

Sales Strategy

(method used to generate sales, reported as a percent of sales dollars)

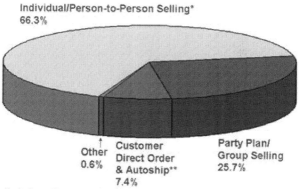

Individual/Person-to-Person Selling*
66.3%

Other
0.6%

Customer
Direct Order
& Autoship**
7.4%

Party Plan/
Group Selling
25.7%

*Including seller personal consumption
**Autoshipments to retail customers of direct sellers

Location of Sales
(reported as a percent of sales dollars)

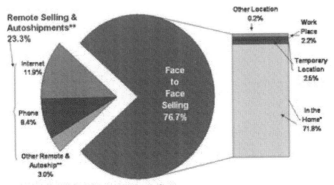

*Including seller personal consumption
**Autoshipments to retail customers of direct sellers

Percent of Sales by Major Product Groups

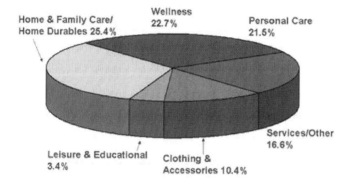

Home/Family Care/Home Durables (cleaning products, cookware, cutlery, etc.)	25.4%
Wellness (weight loss products, vitamins, etc.)	22.7%
Personal Care (cosmetics, jewelry, skin care, etc.)	21.5%
Services/other	16.6%
Clothing & Accessories	10.4%
Leisure/Educational (books, videos, toys, etc.)	3.4%

Age (from 2008 National Sales Force Survey)

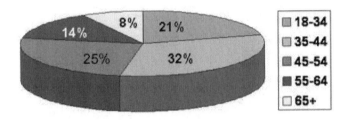

This DSA 2008 National Sales Force Survey is very self explanatory. It simply shows that the Network Marketing industry is an equal employer, and it does not matter how old you are. If you believe you can do it, and you are at least 18 years old, you can do it. What is striking but not surprising is that the 35-54 year age group is when most people get involved. That makes sense because that is when most are seriously looking to situate their finances.

Marital Status (from 2008 National Sales Force Survey)

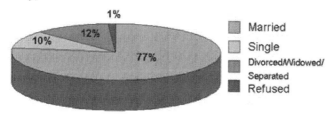

What is revealing and shocking, and I did not know this until I starting writing this book and researching the industry, is that a whopping 77% of those who are involved in network marketing are married. I don't know why. I thought it would be the other way around. I guess it may be that the married people have more mouths to feed. I simply don't know why it is so, but I find it fascinating.

Education (from 2008 National Sales Force Survey)

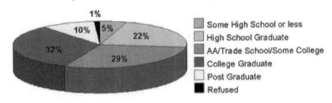

Hours Spent on Direct Selling Per Week
(from 2008 National Sales force Survey)

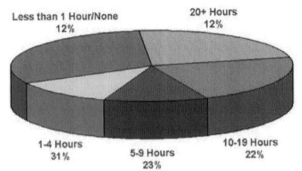

This shows that network marketing is the most flexible business you can run because the pie chart here shows that people simply decide the amount of time without pressure that they want to put into the networking marketing businesses of their choice. It seems though that the most amount of time some put in weekly is 10-19 hours. That is very good. When you compare that time with the hours people put into the traditional business (Me, Myself and I, Inc., and the double-duty employees), you can see it pays off, because you don't have to work as much to earn a reasonable income from this if you find the right one for you and stay the course to achieve your aim.

Estimated 2000 U.S. Retail Sales: $25.57 Billion (source DSA)

Billions of Dollars

1991 $12.96 · 1992 $14.10 · 1993 $14.98 · 1994 $16.55 · 1995 $17.94 · 1996 $20.84 · 1997 $22.21 · 1998 $23.17 · 1999 $24.54 · 2000 $25.57

Estimated 2000 U.S. Salespeople: 11.0 Million (source DSA)

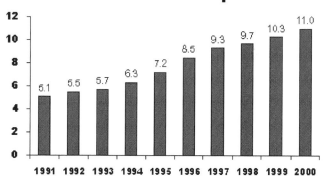

Millions of People

Percent of Sales by Major Product Groups
(source DSA)

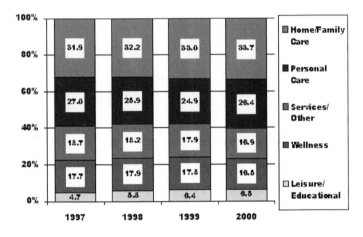

Home/Family Care Products (cleaning products, cookware, cutlery, etc.)	33.7%
Personal Care Products (cosmetics, jewelry, skin care, etc.)	26.4%
Services/other	16.9%
Wellness	16.5%
Leisure/Educational	6.5%

Location of Sales (reported as a percent of sales dollars)

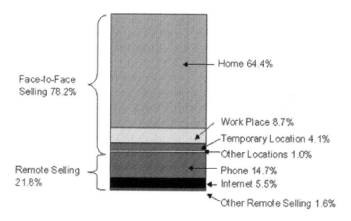

Face-to-Face Selling	78.2%
In the home	64.4%
Workplace	8.7%
Temporary location	4.1%
Other locations	1.0%
Remote Selling	21.8%
Phone	14.7%
Internet	5.5%
Other remote selling	1.6%

~In life and business, you don't get what you want or deserve, but what you <u>negotiate</u> and <u>make happen</u>!~

Sales Strategy (method used to generate sales, reported as a percent of sales dollars)

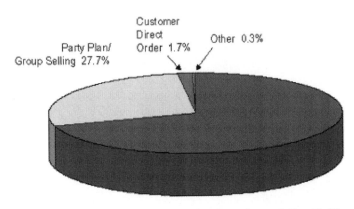

Individual/Person-to-Person selling	70.3%
Party plan/group selling	27.7%
Customer placing order directly with firm (in follow-up to a face-to-face solicitation)	1.7%
Other	0.3%

Compensation Structure by Percent of Firms
(multilevel vs. single level)

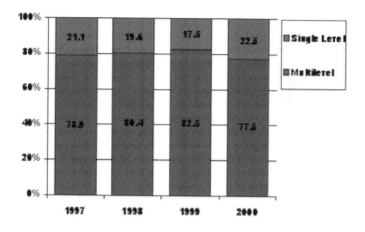

Percent of firms   77.5%/22.5%

Compensation Structure by Percent of Sales Dollars (multilevel vs. single level)

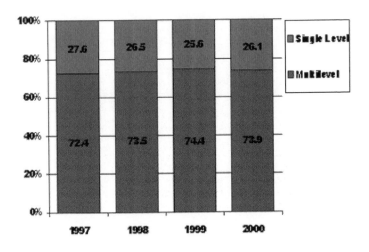

Percent of sales dollars   73.9%/26.1%

Compensation Structure by Percent of Salespeople (multilevel vs. single level)

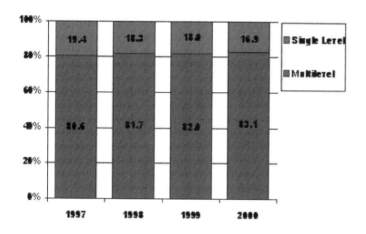

Percent of salespeople   83.1%/16.9%

Gender

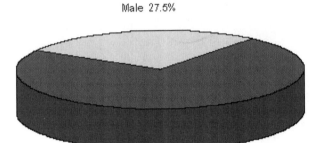

Male 27.5%

Female 72.5%

I am not surprised at these statistics. I believe that women have a more open mind and are more willing to take chances than men. The percentage of women in network marketing is 72.5% while the percentage of men is 27.5%. This may sound sexiest, but it is the truth as you can see from the chart above. Some men say that women are just simply more vulnerable than men. Okay, let's say for the sake of argument that I agree that women are more susceptible to

~In life and business, you don't get what you want or deserve, but what you negotiate and make happen!~

60

doing network marketing than men. Here is my take on it. I would rather be susceptible and take a chance that has the potential to change my life than sit and wonder what could have been. No wonder then that women are taking over the marketplace today.

Age

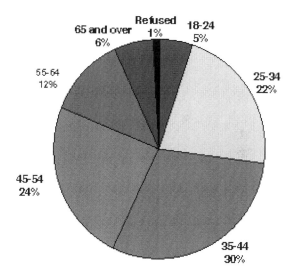

Marital Status

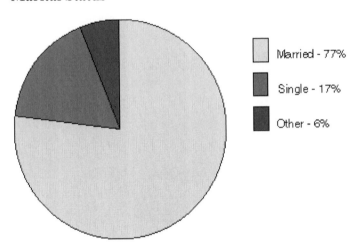

Married - 77%

Single - 17%

Other - 6%

Education

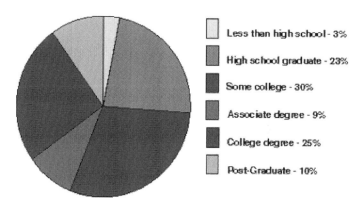

Less than high school - 3%

High school graduate - 23%

Some college - 30%

Associate degree - 9%

College degree - 25%

Post-Graduate - 10%

These statistics are mind blowing and completely shatter the typical stereotype out there that it is the non-educated that become involved in network marketing. From the above statistics, you can see that a resounding 30% have some college education, 25% have a college degree, and of those with less than a high school education, only 3% do network marketing. This makes perfect sense because to be successful in this industry, you need to understand the dynamics involved and have appreciation for what is at stake here.

These facts go to show that most people who reject the industry under the pretense that they are "holier than thou," have it all wrong and need to get over their sweet little selves and take another look at this awesome industry for what it can do for them and their families.

This also goes to show that the more education you have, the more likely it is that you'll get better success with the industry – contrary to the stereotypes out there. This does not mean that you have to have education to be successful in this business. You do not – because I've seen a good number of people with less than proper education do very well in this industry from my former company. So, anyone can do this business. All they need to do is to be *open-minded, coachable and know how to follow a system*. For some, all they need by way of qualification is to have a PHD (Poor, Hungry and Driven) when they come in and get an MBA (Massive Bank Account) when they graduate, which is contrary to how most graduate after a four year college education or higher.

Independent Contractors/Employees

Employees 0.2%

Independent Contractors 99.8%

The reason for this is not farfetched. Employees tend to be complacent and content with the status quo of employment because after all, "I have a good job," which oftentimes for most is an illusion because every day their financial state remains the same or even gets worse, and one negative shift with that position can often devastate their financial freedom. This fact was evidenced with the recent economic burst that left a lot of employees with no other means of income. With the advent of the recession, that trend is changing, and more regular employees that would not have paid attention to network marketing, are now doing it or are taking a look at the opportunity.

No wonder then that a whopping 99.8% of those who do network marketing are independent contractors or independent business owners, and only 2% of regular employees do network marketing. However, this mentality of some employees who say, "I don't need it because I have a good job," is rapidly changing because with the dawn of the sudden meltdown of the marketplace, they now understand the importance of having ***multiple streams of income*** using such opportunities like network marketing that is very inexpensive in most cases to start as a backup source of income or as a means to diversify a small home-based business; not necessarily having multiple jobs.

Hours per week

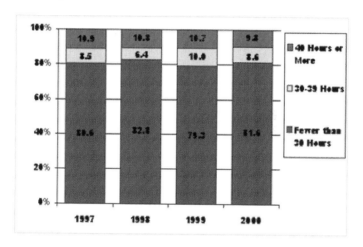

Less than 30 hours per week   81.6%/8.6%/9.8%
30-39/40 or more

Average Percent of Time Spent on...

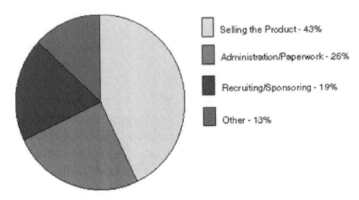

Selling the Product - 43%

Administration/Paperwork - 25%

Recruiting/Sponsoring - 19%

Other - 13%

This chart simply shows that anyone with any lifestyle or work schedule can do network marketing because the hours are very flexible and you put in the hours you want and when you want. That spells FREEDOM and not BONDAGE!

Main Reason for Becoming A Direct Sales Representative

Additional income	32%
Believe in the product/good product	20%
Discount/wholesale/free products	10%
Liked the presentation/organization/people	3%
Be able to stay at home with children/parent	3%
Personally use the product	3%
Flexibility	3%
Asked by relative	3%
To be able to get the product more easily	3%
Other	20%

This data shows that people do network marketing for varying reasons. This is **why** we say in this industry that your **reason** or **why** for getting into the business will determine your height of success.

What is the primary reason you became a direct seller? (source DSA)

- To earn supplemental income
- To earn full-time income
- To buy the products I like at a discount
- To meet other people
- I like to be recognized for my accomplishments

FAST FACTS ABOUT DIRECT SELLING
(source DSA)

70%	of sellers have been with their company 1+ years
80%	of sellers say direct selling meets or exceeds their expectations

85%	of sellers report a good, very good or excellent experience with direct selling
74%	of U.S. adults have purchased products from a direct seller
15.1 million	people in the U.S. are involved in direct selling
$29.6 billion	in total U.S. sales
$114 billion	sales worldwide

Percent of Salespeople by Distributorship Type

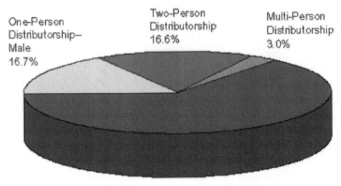

One-person distributorship: female	63.7%
One-person distributorship: male	16.7%
Two-person distributorship	16.6%
Multi-person distributorship	3.0%

Hours per week

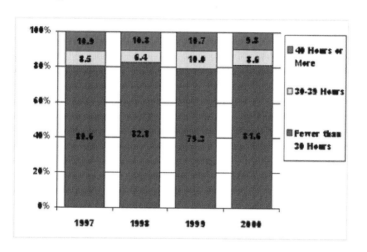

Less than 30 hours per week   81.6%/8.6%/9.8%
30-39/40 or more

What the Moguls in the Industry are Saying About Network Marketing

If someone wants to go into business, isn't the first thing they do is find out what the experts in that field are saying and doing? The answer is yes. Here then, are what some of the moguls and experts are saying about network marketing.

Both Robert Kiyosaki, the author of "Rich Dad, Poor Dad," and real estate mogul Donald Trump, have attested that if they had to do it over again, they would do network marketing. It has also been established that Warren Buffet (Pampered Chef), the third richest man in the world, has earned a fortune from Direct Sales (which is tantamount to network marketing).

Network marketing or direct selling allows you to create your financial freedom like no other business opportunity does today in the marketplace, because of the intrinsic leveraging capability as opposed to laboring and earning income linearly, which is with very intense labor and often without much reward either immediately or later on. It also incorporates singularity of effort as opposed to MLM that adopts and embraces leveraging which can lead to massive wealth creation in time.

In fact, Donald Trump has a new network organization called "The Trump Network." Being a very savvy businessman, Donald Trump knew what kind of financial fortune can come from network marketing. In fact, Trump said, "I believe in network marketing." Another exact quote from Trump on the issue of network marketing and why everyone should consider it is, "It is time for all of us to diversify our assets and take back the American Dream." – *Donald J. Trump*

The Damage Network Marketing Can Do to Your Life and Business and How to Restore Them

1. Psychological damage

Let's take a look at the definition of the word **psychology** because if you understand the etymology of the word, it helps you know how to apply it to bring about the change you want. According to the *Encarta Dictionary*: psychology (noun) can be defined as follows:

Study of human mind: the scientific study of the human mind and mental states and of human and animal behavior. The study of it tells us that if you understand the mindset of anyone you are about to sell or market or present something to, you are more likely to succeed than not to achieve. You must first establish some kind of connection or relationship with the person beforehand even if it is someone you just met. There are ways to connect with someone you just met and still sell to them successfully. This is another subject matter for another book.

a. **Characteristic mental makeup:** the characteristic temperaments and associated behavior of a person or group, or that exhibited by those engaged in any activity. This goes to show that if your thinking faculty is wrong, your physical effort will not amount to much. It is not all about hard work; it is both hard work and smart work which are embedded in the psychology of presentation and marketing.

If you want to succeed in direct sales or marketing in general, there are *5 critical principal mindset ingredients that must be adopted with the <u>mindset</u> of all sales persons if they are to become 'great' sales persons:*

- **Change your presentation mindset – change your presentation result.**
- **Change your presentation style – change your life!**
- **Change your presentation style – change your money!**
- **Change your presentation style – change your destiny!**
- **Change your presentation acumen – change your vision.**

b. **Subtle manipulative behavior:** subtle clever actions and words used to influence a person or group.

I will be the first to put a disclaimer on this topic from a qualification standpoint because I am not speaking here as a qualified psychologist. However, this book will be inconsequential from all perspectives if the psychological aspects of the issues here are not addressed because we all know by now that marketing or selling is more of a mental mindset than anything else. What I find in this industry is that people psych-up (size up) others psychologically.

I have opined time and again that success in marketing, sales and/or presentation of any service or product or any matter is won or lost in both mental and environmental psychology more than any other factor involved in sales such as the product or service. This is why people with very poor self-esteem do not do well in business until they change their mental set-up or mentality and perform differently.

Over the years, as I gained stronger ground in speaking, presenting, marketing and sales, more people began to inquire as to how I do it and do it successfully. Then I began to examine why most cannot present their subject matter and get the intended result. Please note that I am talking about the "batting rate" of the sales person using the totality of circumstance. This does not mean that I get a "yes" in every single presentation or sale that I conduct. It means that the more times I get my way and the more successful I get, the more guts I have to dare to go to the next level. This again goes to show that success is progressive and incremental just like faith is incremental and progressive and not a sudden windfall. It also means that you have to start to be good. You have to be bad to be good. You have to be good to be great and you have to be great to be awesome.

Psychology of Presentations we make every day without knowing the impact that you need to be mindful of:

- Do you know that the way you smile, laugh, stand, frown, dance, talk, walk, work, shake hands, show confidence or lack thereof, etc. are forms of presentations?

- Do you know that the way you carry yourself, your posture; the way you position yourself or not is a form of presentation?

- Do you know that the problem may not lie in the business or opportunity but in your way of presentation or lack thereof? And some even allow themselves to be held hostage by their pasts...and much more!!!!!!!!

In order to drive the point home here, let me start with a dictionary definition of the word 'psychology'. Here are a few definitions (source – *Encarta Dictionary – North America*):

A. Guess somebody's thought processes: to guess or anticipate correctly the intentions or thoughts of another person. Let's start with the first definition, which is to "guess somebody's thought processes."

I just finished a fantastic workshop on a topic called, "How to present anything effectively and successfully, to anybody, any day, anywhere and everywhere without fear and intimidation." During this presentation, I talked at length on the psychology of presentation.

In making any presentation to anyone effectively and successfully, you must have the *art* and *gift* of being able to perceive or guess somebody's thought process. I never say anything to anyone without first knowing 99.9% of the time what I will get in return. If you don't have it, learn it because it is a soft skill, if you are serious about succeeding in anything that you do because life is full of series of presentations even if you don't know that you are presenting daily. Your ability to make this assessment will greatly improve your return on your investment in the marketplace.

What I've found out and what most people in this industry do not know is that every potential customer or business partner out there does not like to buy or join a business partner who is not even sure of and believe in what in the world they are talking about or what they are trying to sell. People are not stupid; they know that you either know what you are talking about or that you don't know what you are talking about. So, don't sign up and not take the time to master your subject matter and meander through the process and expect people to believe you and help you succeed.

Other people can sense whether you have confidence and whether you are enthused about what you are trying to share with them. In the MLM industry it has been established that "ignorance on fire will always outperform knowledge on ice." So, if you are not enthused and excited about what you are about, you might as well not bother because your prospects will see through that, and you will not succeed.

Here is what I say, "I would rather have some of the information and be enthused and excited about however much I know and move on that passionately in the marketplace and learn the rest along the way, than have tons of information but have no enthusiasm and confidence in what it is. If the enthusiasm and confidence is not there, your success rate is highly minimized. We all now know that *"ignorance on fire will always outperform knowledge on ice."* Note that people would have to accept your physiological appearances and utterances before they ask to know more of what you've got to offer.

B. **Intimidate somebody:** to intimidate somebody or undermine the confidence of somebody.

C. **Puzzle something out:** to analyze, solve, or understand something such as a problem.

2. Emotional damage

I am sure someone already is asking, "What does emotion have to do in the place of business?" Well, I am glad you asked. Even though in the business world they preach that you should remove your emotions away from doing business, I'm here to say I've tried it and quickly found out that there is a direct correlation between our emotions and how we conduct our daily affairs – yes, even in business.

Well let's start by explaining in plain terms what emotion is. Emotion is simply another word for "feeling." How many people would say even in their respective dealings in business that their **emotion** or **feeling** is completely removed from the equation? So, here is my point; whether you like it or not, a lot of people will get your emotions aroused to the point that they will get you upset because they act in ways you have never known before or even worse, contrary to what you know to be the way people should conduct themselves in the marketplace.

~In life and business, you don't get what you want or deserve, but what you <u>negotiate</u> and <u>make happen</u>!~

Therefore, if you are not emotionally sound or not strong enough to make sure that those unscrupulous people in the network market do not push you so hard that you allow your emotions to outweigh your business objectives, you will quit because of it. I know for a fact that a lot of people from the previous company I was with for a long time as well as the company I was with briefly, quit because they could not take the emotional roller coaster and ballet. It became and would always be the survival of the most emotionally strong and mentally astute because a lot of unstable individuals and "Network Junkies" have no rules to play by and do not adhere to the rules of engagement.

The point

Here is my point. If you know that the situation or business opportunity you've become involved with definitely is the one for you, would you let other people who came for the exact same reason you came, run you off?

~In life and business, you don't get what you want or deserve, but what you <u>negotiate</u> and <u>make happen</u>!~

Knowing that business is war, and the emotional, spiritual, mental and other clashes you will go through are the battles in the war, would you quit just because of someone else's idiosyncrasies? As for me, those kinds of unprofessional and unethical behaviors actually bring out the genius in me and basically make me swear to succeed, because those who come at you in this way – intended for you to vanish – do so especially if they feel that you are a threat because of their insecurities and not understanding that there is enough money for everyone. This statement that I am making here is a very bold one. If you ask people in the industry, some will agree and some will not. Their answers depend on which side of the fence they are on and whether they are the dispensers or the recipients of the attitude.

My recommendation

It does not matter whether you were emotionally sound or not before you got involved in the business. If you really believe in the opportunity that the business will afford you, you should be willing to go through the mental and emotional challenges that you will surely encounter because everywhere you go there will be people. Like in any other business, there are strong-minded and well-intentioned people. There are also those who are callous who would do anything for money and success.

You should hang in there, re-strategize on how you will defeat them and not quit so you'll get your portion. We all know by now, it goes without saying that "whatever is worth having is worth fighting for," and that "without change and challenge, long-lasting change is only a dream." Making that decision will help you grow in every sense of the word, in more ways than one – emotionally, mentally, financially, spiritually and much more. I do believe that "that which does not kill you will make you stronger and better." You don't get bitter, but you get better.

I normally take different approaches to achieve my goals when I encounter those kinds of unscrupulous situations or people. This is what I do. I quickly pull back to examine the situation by asking myself the following questions:

(a) Does this business still make financial sense for me? Or is it time to look elsewhere?

(b) If the answer to the first question is "yes", then how do I change my strategies to make sure what happened does not happen again and that I'm still positioned to get my portion?

(c) Do these people have the power to run me out of my position? For me, the answer is "no"; however, I know the power of "once bitten, twice shy." I am much convicted on integrity, and when I find that the people do not exude it in the way they carry themselves, I make changes immediately and give them a new boundary. And yet I still wax very strong on my own solid ground of what I want without letting those people push me out of my post.

The amazing thing is that each and every time someone tries to come at me with evil intent or jealousy, God always turns it around for my good. This is because I have come to realize that if you have a rest in God in all that you do, you will have restful increase and not stressful increase. This type of increase that I am talking about often comes to those who understand that we are blessed not because we labor, but rather we labor because we are blessed. If you are already personally and professionally seasoned and developed, you may not experience this problem. So this part is not for you. Pay it forward to those who may need to learn it.

I thought I was personally developed before I came into the industry; however, I found to the contrary that I had a lot of work to do and I think that overall it was good for me, because as a result, I am stronger today and more poised to succeed than I was five years ago. Right now I consider myself as fire and no other fire can burn me unless I choose to subdue myself. It made me realize that the best revenge in life is living well and gaining success. To live and succeed well requires that you know who you are and whose you are and have the strategy to succeed!

If it signals to me that my time is up in a particular endeavor, and it is time to go, does that mean that the thing that I came to get should be forgotten? Or does it simply mean that I need to look for another vehicle to accomplish the goal in a new environment?

A lot of people do not understand that change of vehicle is not failure. The time you fail is when you stop "trying." Sometimes change is the only thing that will bring you closer to your success. I found that out when my husband and I left the first network company that we had joined, had attained a substantial success at and had become Senior Vice President of that company in record time too.

(d) Do you know that sometimes you may be carrying a load but not know it and accidently you stumble upon a stone and the load falls off, and you suddenly feel very light and relieved and wonder how come you did not realize that you were carrying such a load? Well that was what happened to us with our previous company.

3. Mental battle/war

Most battles in life and business are often won or lost mentally. Physical fight is often seen as a barbaric act except in times of war where it is warranted. The best fight is with mental and pen power. If you have your brain intact and can think critically, you don't need to fight with anybody physically regardless of the issue. I personally prefer mental war because I know for a fact that you can use your mind to defeat and restructure where the enemies would not know how to act. Most people are not afraid of a physical fight, but most are very afraid of mental war because they don't know what you are thinking and what you are up to; that can scare the hell out of them.

If you are mentally astute, you will not allow anyone to outsmart you and push you out of your destiny. You don't have anything to prove to anybody by exchanging words. Rather, focus and shift your thinking toward money-making time (MMT) because at the end of the day that is what really matters when you are in business. After all, the best revenge in life is living well and attaining success.

4. Lies and more lies

Some people tell me that one of the reasons why they do not like network marketing is because a lot of people lie to their business partners. Let's face it; anywhere people are gathered for a common goal or cause, misunderstanding is bound to happen because no matter what you do, you are bound to meet disgruntled people in every business or place of work. So, that is not a disturbing fact in network marketing. You will find it everywhere there are people. All you need to do is make sure that you are not one of the people perpetuating the lies and innuendos and stay focused on your mission.

Here is the point or lesson to learn from here. If you cannot change the people around you and the people you are around, then you must change the group of people you currently associate with and cultivate a new group that possesses what you are looking for. Whatever you focus on will expand, and what you don't feed will die. Choose not to be part of it, and it will not impact on you and your business. You must remember that the strength in you will bring out the weakness in others, and they will hate you for it. Soon after, they will begin to conjure up stories and lies about you just to distract you from your goal and focus. Ignore them and stand your ground – PERIOD!

5. Intimidation/fear of loss at play

They were all trying to intimidate us. They thought we would give up and not finish the work. But God made me strong. Nehemiah 6:9

One of the quick lessons I learned when I first got into network marketing is that a lot of the so-called leaders try to size you up and check you out to see if they can intimidate you and subdue you instead of adding you to the leadership. Be very careful who you align with and who you trust. First, you must test them with small things, and in time and in some instances it does not take long to figure them out.

"Be courteous to all, be intimate with few, and let that few be tried before you give them your confidence." – George Washington

If you do not have a good spirit of discernment, you may get bitten before you know it. That bite does not have to be fatal unless you let it. All you need to do is learn very quickly from it, but do not retract from your objective. Rather, regroup, re-strategize and restructure and go again. Don't quit because you are disappointed because that big elephant on your back (not being financially free) has not dropped off. You must continue on your quest until you arrive. Remember also that *"in your journey through life, there are many tempting parking spaces, but you must not park until you get to your final destination."*

6. Low self-esteem

Low self-esteem is a bigger problem than most people would care to admit. Low self-esteem comes from our thought process concerning our environment and what is or is not happening that we may like or don't like and that affects us negatively in how we view ourselves in comparison to others. It is, in some cases, the reason for jealousy, hate and wickedness.

What killed it for me was a simple but very powerful quote by one of the First Ladies of the United States of America – Eleanor Roosevelt. She said: "*No one can make you feel inferior without your permission.*" Think about this statement for a second and see if you get it. Here is what I took away from the quote. Whenever I come around ANYONE, it is entirely up to me to decide whether to allow them to intimidate me psychologically with what they do or do not do with my "consent" or my permission.

That means I have a role to play in how I allow others' idiosyncrasies or dispositions affect or not affect me. So, let no one intimidate you for any reason. They came into this world in pursuit of the very same thing that you came into this world to pursue. So, give yourself the permission to stand firm in your post and get your reward. *You must stick and stay until you get your pay.* No one's life is better than yours, unless you tell yourself that. *Remember that perception is reality.* The mind game is HEAVY and serious in this business. So beware, be prepared and be in control of your mind and guard it with all your might. It is your most important asset!

7. Loss of self confidence and ability to achieve

Whatever you do, never allow your confidence in yourself and what you believe in to be tampered with by anyone. There are certain characteristics of successful people in business and in life, and healthy self-esteem and confidence is one of them. The truth is that if you lack confidence in yourself and what you are marketing or sharing, you will never succeed. Most of the time, people are not technically buying the product/services you bring before them. They are buying into you. If they are not into you, they could care less what else you have to offer. You first must sell yourself, and they must see and believe that you are confident in what you are presenting.

~In life and business, you don't get what you want or deserve, but what you <u>negotiate</u> and <u>make happen</u>!~

If you lose self confidence in your ability to achieve in life or in business, you might as well forget it. Everything you achieve or don't achieve in life or business starts with your belief system and mindset, both of which rely heavily upon healthy self-esteem and confidence.

8. Constant promise and fail by the company

A lot of people who tried network marketing and quit have also been disillusioned from the constant promise and fail that permeate the industry. In many instances, the problem may not even lie with the company or products and services, but **YOU!**

Sometimes it is not intended by the companies to promise and fail, and at other times the unscrupulous ones meant to defraud or intended to from the onset. However, you cannot discount the whole industry just because a few have done wrong. Network marketing is not for the faint (weak) of heart.

Everywhere you go in life and business, there will be deceitful and unscrupulous people, and this will continue for as long as the earth remains. Just make sure you are not one of them and that you live as cleanly, ethically and professionally as possible, and your payday is around the corner if it is not in your mailbox right now.

9. There are a lot of mean people in the industry – devise a strategy to outsmart them and succeed

Restructuring, regrouping and reorganizing is not failing. **In fact, it is essential for success.**

I've found out that there are a lot of disgruntled and disenfranchised people in network marketing that further propagate the negative reputation that the industry has garnered over time. When you get into network marketing, you should quickly make up your mind that you are not there for any other reason or person, but you are there to make money in as honest a manner as you can. You will surely encounter the mean-spirited, unethical and selfish and unscrupulous people who would make you question your decision to get involved in the first place. However, you must not allow yourself to think too long on that path because it can divert or even worse, divorce you from the point or reason for getting involved, *which is to change your family's financial well-being generationally.*

Don't lose sight of what is important and do not allow yourself to major in the minor and minor in the major. All you need to do is re-strategize, re-group, re-think, re-organize and re-position yourself at your post, and do so this time more intelligently than the first time.

10. Have your own game plan on how you are going to make it

A lot of people today still do not get it that success is strategy and planning. You all know the famous quote that says, *"If you fail to plan, you plan to fail."* Someone once said, "the harder you work, the luckier you get." I would say, the more prepared you are, the quicker God will put you in a position that would reward you for your faith and hard work. The more prepared you are, the luckier you will get – even though it has been established that luck is where preparation meets opportunity. If you are not prepared when the opportunity comes, the opportunity will seem like trash to you. That is why they say, one man's meat is another man's poison and that opportunities do not go away, they simply go to those that are ready!

"Many products are sold by network markets, also known as direct sales, network marketing or consumer direct marketing..." "Business opportunities" crop up in backyard cookout conversations in as many varieties as barbeque sauce recipes. The key to success...is to recruit other people to sell it well.

Nationwide, multi-level marketers sell $30 billion a year of telecommunication devices, legal services, cosmetics, nutritional supplements and a myriad of other products. Worldwide, the market exceeds $111 billion, according to the Direct Selling Association.
– The Washington Post, July 9, 2009

My projection

I will even dare to project that network marketing in the near future will be the way we do business or how major chains will choose to move their products and services to the end users. This projection is based largely on what has happened in the marketplace with this industry since the recession with the outburst of many companies that have dabbled in the industry. Another reason is that so many more people since the recession who were shocked and are still shocked about how high and dry they were left with no alternatives of making money are now seeing network marketing as a possible means or additional alternative means of a multiple stream of income.

Some other views on network marketing

"In a typical multi-level marketing model, less than one percent of people who become involved in sales and recruitment make enough to cover their investment in products and operating expenses," according to Jon Taylor, a former multi-level marketing sales representative and founder of the Consumer Awareness Institute, an industry watchdog group. "Up to 90 percent of the commissions are distributed to less than 1 percent of all participants – those at or near the top, with a big chunk going to company founders," Taylor says. **If Jon Taylor's base premise is correct, does that necessarily mean that it is the fault of the industry? Or is that the way it is in most cases?**

Here again, I am defending the direct sales industry. Does everyone at the corporate level earn the same amount of money? The answer is emphatically and resoundingly NO! A case in point is what has been reported about the unconscionable and unfathomable amount of bonuses that the top corporate executives on Wall Street have been racking up against the general interest of the main street who seem to do the bulk of the hard labor. Information and research has it that most of those at the Wall Street level who take home most of the money are busy having and basking in the finest sunshines of the world, while the main street level labors. Again keeping things in their proper perspectives, the point here is that most are quick to condemn and generalize because they don't like the industry without further investigation or analysis.

11. Ponzi scheme at its worst

If you take a close look at the case of the famous and notorious Ponzi scam committed by Bernard Madoff, which for all intents and purposes was not supposed to be a network marketing scheme; however, under the umbrella and open eye of Wall Street he took all his investors to the cleaners and committed the worst scam in the history of Ponzi schemes. This is how Yahoo described it: **"***Bernard Lawrence 'Bernie' Madoff is a former stock broker, investment adviser, non-executive chairman of the NASDAQ stock market, and the admitted operator of what has been described as the largest <u>Ponzi scheme</u> in history.***"**

First of all, what is a Ponzi scheme or Pyramid?

A lot of people get stuck on the word "Pyramid," and, based on stereotype or bad experience with such a **business structure**, they lose sight of what is important and totally miss what a pyramidal business structure can afford. They are not even aware of other pyramidal structured systems such as any place of employment (where you have the CEO, Vice-President, Manager, Supervisor, team leader, secretary, all the way to the butler and the cleaners of the buildings) that they have been associated with, but never thought about what that structure is because society does not frown on it. If you picture what I just shared right now, you will see a pyramid

– starting with the CEO on top. So, get over the nomenclature and see what network marketing can do for you and yours.

Definition of Pyramid

Here are a few definitions from *Encarta Dictionary* of what a pyramid is: (a) a solid triangular shape that has triangular sides that slope to meet in a point and base; (b) a system with expanding structure – an arrangement or system that has a small number of items at one point and expands gradually to have a large number at the opposite point; (3) Investment method – FINANCE: a financial risk structure that spreads investments between high, medium, and low risk.

With the definition of what a pyramid scheme is, it is safe to say that a pyramid is simply the shape of a structure, like rectangle or sphere, except that it is used here as a business module that some business owners use to bring new products and services to the marketplace and that avails ordinary, everyday people exceptional opportunities to get a chance to earn extraordinary income from minimal turnkey investment. That is why the module is shaped triangularly. The original promoter(s) starts the process and thereafter opens it up to the mass of ordinary people who would not otherwise have been able to invest in such an expensive business venture.

Most structures in life and business are shaped pyramidally. Therefore, it is safe for me to state at this juncture that the problem with this scheme is not in the nomenclature, but rather in the intended purpose and how those who form the structure use it. Some form the structure for good use and others with bad intentions. Just because there are a few bad apples that have used the structure for their own selfish purposes, this should not negate the fact that the structure can be used for good like in the case of PHPI. This endorsement of PHPI does not mean that PHPI is perfect because it is not, just as nothing in life is perfect. It is just that for now PHPI is the only company that I believe epitomizes the good that can come from the pyramid structure that many despise just because of one bad experience or bias or common stereotypes.

Classic Ponzi or pyramid scheme

There is, of course, illegal use of the concept which brings me to the classic Ponzi scheme or pyramid that has left a bad taste in a lot of peoples' mouths. This is part of the reason why many people who would have gravitated to the industry, shy away from it just because they are not informed about the distinction between the two. Let's examine what a Ponzi scheme is and how it is different from a legal pyramid.

What is a Ponzi scheme?

A Ponzi scheme is a fraudulent investment operation that pays returns to separate investors from their own money or money paid by subsequent investors, rather than from any actual profit earned. The Ponzi scheme usually entices new investors by offering returns other investments cannot guarantee, in the form of short-term returns that are either abnormally high or unusually consistent. – Yahoo Search

Ponzi scheme started by Charles Ponzi *(March 3, 1882 - January 18, 1949), an Italian swindler, who is considered one of the greatest swindlers in American history. His aliases include **Charles Ponei, Charles P. Bianchi, Carl** and **Carlo**. The term "Ponzi scheme" is a widely known description of any scam that pays early investors returns from the investments of later investors. He promised clients a 50% profit within 45 days, or 100% profit within 90 days, by buying discounted postal reply coupons in other countries and redeeming them at face value in the United States as a form of arbitrage.* – from Wikipedia, the free encyclopedia and Yahoo Search

"Multilevel marketing, which includes legitimate companies as well as illegal schemes, *tends to grow when the economy sours and people lose their jobs or fear they will. The Direct Selling Association, a D.C.-based industry trade group whose members include companies such as Quixtar (formerly*

Amway) ... reports that membership has spiked during the last two recessions." – The Washington Post of July 9, 2009

This Washington Post article of July 9, 2009 goes on to bolster my point that every business has the potential to be infiltrated by con artists all the while being promoted as legitimate businesses. So the same types of unscrupulous and egregious behaviors that occur in the conventional marketplace also are obtainable in the network marketing or direct selling industry. So, don't get hung up on the label or stereotypes, but rather look beyond the label to see if it is Ponzi or non-Ponzi.

12. Choose your primary partners strategically, carefully, have a mind of your own, and don't let them draw you in to the point of no return

Here is what I mean. There are many people in this situation, but to elucidate my point, I am going to use the case of someone whom I will call "Jan" that I met in the network marketing business.

Using "Jan" as an example of point of no return (poor)

In a series of conversations with "Jan", I found out that she has been in a certain network marketing business for over two years, and faithfully I might add. Every painful month she pays out-of-pocket to support the system deficiency to support her *up line* so that her *up line* will not fall from their top positions. She expressed to me that she is desperate about the situation but that hopefully one day she will make it. (*Here again PHPI can be distinguished from this company's unfavorable compensation plan because with PHPI, you don't have to worry about anyone falling from the top back down to the bottom – ever).* My question to "Jan" was – how?

Mind you, "Jan" does not make a penny of her own from this company; she only has a couple of recruits, and at this point she admits that she is **bleeding heavily financially**. It did not make sense to me that anyone would let themselves be put in such an unconscionable position for that length of time.

I asked "Jan" why she didn't let it go and look for another profitable network opportunity out there that would not involve her becoming bankrupt financially and emotionally as a result. I am sure that where she found herself was not what she had intended when she signed up to become involved in the business. "Jan" hesitated for a while before answering. When she finally answered, she told me that her up lines had told her that she could not disconnect her credit card from the system because they are depending on her to stand and maintain their positions. She did not want to be the one who burst the bubble. So, she stayed to her detriment. Note here that there is a fine line but powerful line between being stupid and being nice.

The fine line between being stupid and being nice!

I explained to "Jan" that there is a small but yet huge fine line between being nice and being stupid. I went on to explain to her that I walked that fine line for years, even to my own detriment, because I did not want people to be mad at me. However, spirituality and self-empowerment are journeys and paths of progressive growth and must be done in time individually. One day I got the aha! moment and I knew when not to cross that 'fine' line. "Jan" told me that what I shared with her made a lot of sense, but she was very afraid of what her up lines would do, and she did not want to be the one that would burst the bubble.

At the end of the day she quivered for a few seconds and said that she was going to pray about it and wait on God to guide her and tell her what to do next.

That was when I drew the line in the sand and told her that she had crossed the line and that she was being stupid. I told her that she should not use the Lord's name in vain because our God is a smart and intelligent God and has given us all the willpower to know right from wrong and that we should not become doormats for others in order to be seen as nice people. It is a business. If you are not making money after a reasonable time, then you are not in business unless you have convinced yourself that you are running a charitable operation or a mere social club.

Note!
"Jan" not making money in this case does not inherently mean that the company she is affiliated with is the culprit. It could be, and/or it could be due to several other factors that I have discussed here in this book. In this case, it could be that "Jan" is simply weak and suffering with the people-pleasing syndrome and is not able to stand up for herself.

It could also be that the company's compensation plan drives the individuals in it to build incorrectly and selfishly, which may be a way to hold people hostage financially with the false hope that someday they will make it. From looking at the facts surrounding this case (that I know all too well), from all indications, it is virtually impossible that "Jan" was going to make anything from it. Now, would you blame the company for "Jan's" state of affairs in this situation?

At this point, I think she now qualifies to be called a network marketing junky. The majority of the junkies never really make money. They simply support the system and become boulders for others to succeed. So, my question for you is which one are you? And considering the fact that you did not make it in your last network marketing business, did you make a decision to make it right, or did you quit and say, "it does not work?"

The point...

Only very few people make the right decision the first time; most make a decision and then right it.

If you make a bad decision initially, it does not have to be fatal unless you allow it to be, and you don't have to quit. You stay the course and in the process make your bad decision right.

13. Leaders should be careful what they say and do to their business partners

Again, using PHPI as a case in point, it really matters what you say to or what you call your business partners. PHPI vehemently rejects such labeling, but rather prefers the terms "support organization" and "leadership." For a long time after I became rooted in the network marketing industry, I was concerned that business associates were called by a demeaning and derogatory name like "down line". And I was not alone in my thought that when people are called a demeaning name or below class name, it does not encourage them or make them feel better about themselves but rather lowers their self-esteem, making them feel worse than they did before joining the organization.

14. Leaders should lead with integrity

The *North American Encarta Dictionary* defines integrity:

- **The possession of firm principles:** as the quality of possessing and steadfastly adhering to high moral principles or professional standards
- **Completeness:** the state of being complete or undivided
- **Wholeness:** the state of being sound or undamaged

Integrity is a state of being. It is doing the right thing when nobody is watching. It is a lifestyle of the inside of your being matching the outward expression. It is living authentically, being trustworthy and honest even in the face of opportunity and temptation and opposition to do anything to the contrary. Based on my findings, unfortunately, a very good percentage of the leaders in the industry lack integrity and honor.

PHPI makes the much-needed change in this department!

One of the things that impressed me about the founder and CEO of PHPI, Derrick Rodgers, is that he said that one of the first things that is inherently wrong with the MLM industry is the demeaning position titles. He told us right off the block that he was not going to have anyone be referred to as a "down line", for example, but rather by a better title such as "support organization" or "leadership organization". It makes perfect sense that people would want to be part of an organization where the name they are called is inclusive and supportive-minded instead of divisive. It has been proven time without number in corporate America that when people feel good or better about themselves, they perform better and treat others with dignity. I could not agree more!

15. MLM does not have time for babysitting

Multi-level marketing does not have time to babysit anyone. What is sad about it is that from my findings, experience, observations, information and research, a very large number of the people who get involved in MLM expect to do nothing and become millionaires. They expect to just sign up and put the responsibly of making it in the business on the person who brought them into the business. That is wrong, and people should cease and desist from such faulty expectations and mentality. You are the President and the CEO of your business, and you should never put the responsibility of the success of your business in the hands of others. It is your business; take charge of it.

A lot of people even think that it is a get-rich-quick scheme, and they expect to make millions overnight. Yes, you can earn money fairly quickly in network business, but you have to put in some work in the beginning. This business is not for the faint of heart who just want to sit and complain, finding every reason to make excuses and finding something wrong or someone to blame for not taking charge of their business. It is your responsibility to succeed. Except for occasional support from your leadership and support organization when you need it, you have to negotiate and make it happen for yourself.

16. Beware of the unscrupulous leaders/representatives

The unscrupulous leaders are the cut-throat leaders that will stop at nothing to get to the top, including psychologically "gaming" their business partners or support organizations by the false advice they give them that has nothing to do with what they need to do especially in the beginning of their businesses. I experienced this heavily from one of the companies I was with previously.

A good number of the leadership on top would tell us – the new members – to buy and put money where we should not have had any business doing so, simply to promote their own selfish interests, only for us to find out too late into the game that it was actually for the leadership's own financial selfish interests. Most of us did not find out that we had been taken advantage of until it was too late into the game. After we realized that the so-called leadership had taken us to the cleaners, we all had just two choices – one, either to get mad and quit; or two, to stay and work hard to flush the loss and gain. Most chose the first and quit and started bad-mouthing the company. I do not know for a fact whether "corporate" was aware of what those so-called leaders were doing and just turned their back or not. For me, there was no turning back. As soon as I figured out their games, I immediately changed my game plan and took charge. I got the deceitful leaders off my business, repositioned myself and then got to the top of the company.

The best way to get even in business is to get even in the marketplace. Anything else is just blabbing, and that would neither give you money nor power.

One of the things that made it so obvious about what their motives were, was that at the same time they were using you to make money and attain another pin level, they would call you day-in-day-out and were very nice and would do anything to be there for you and even call you the sweetest name in the dictionary for the moment, and as soon as they didn't need you, you were tossed to the side and they looked for the next target. Based on the compensation structure of that company, people became very dishonest and self-centered and did anything just to make it. In fact, I am convinced that this fact contributed heavily to the mass exodus of representatives from that company. *However, one of my specialties is knowing how to turn a bad situation into a good thing and into profit.* So, I did and the rest is history.

17. Beware of the "backyardigans" of MLM

Beware of the all-around players in the industry. The "backyardigans" are those who come in front of you and say one thing pleasing and behind you they stab you. These are the unstable and dishonest people who try to play everyone, and in the end they've played themselves, because at some point it catches up with them and their center will fall apart before they realize that they did not play anyone but themselves. I saw and still see a lot of these types of unacceptable, unprofessional and unethical behaviors in the industry.

Am I saying that it will not happen here at PHPI? No, because wherever you have people, there will always be disagreements. However, the magnitude and the levels and the impunity with which those people carried on with these unethical and unprofessional conducts was so blatant and brazen that most people began to exit the system, which led to the downfall of many and had negative impact on the company's pocketbook and reputation.

18. Favoritism/nepotism/racism are the silent killers in the industry

They hope they can get you to bring your people and then dispose of you as they need – but not this one – on my own terms ONLY!

Let's get this fact out of the way: favoritism and all the other "isms" will never end for as long as the earth remains. So, don't get all worked up and quit, even though it is a very painful thing to go through. Rather, when you encounter them in the process, *find creative ways to overcome and still get your portion. Realize that no one can stop you but YOU!*

Having been there and done that, I found the perfect network marketing leaders who do not tolerate the scheme that I explained here in terms of the different "isms" that permeate certain network companies which I found often led to their own downward spirals. Some of the people that I met at PHPI like Betty Miles, Richard Pressley and Beth Hinson Phillips, to mention but a few, work very hard to make sure that they play fair with everyone to the best of their abilities so no one feels left out.

Ms. Beth Henson Phillips, whom I have dubbed "the mother of PHPI," and Betty Miles, epitomize the ideal leadership qualities you want in your leaders. Ms. Betty Miles, in her comment on this book, said, *"I think there is a tremendous need for honesty and transparency when reviewing and analyzing the pros and cons of network marketing! There is a difficult struggle ahead of us if we are to gain the credibility we desire!! We must take the high road of integrity rather than the low one of expediency."* Each and every time I speak to them and see how they treat others with respect and honor, I remain in awe as to the degree of integrity they exude from the heart, and the professional and fair ways from which they operate.

I am confident that this is who they are because I had an opportunity to publicly observe them without them knowing I was doing so with the general public during the prelaunch of PHPI when people swamped them – some people they knew and those they did not know. If you are not told, you would think they were all friends by the way they sincerely and passionately hugged, kissed and cared for all in the group. Note though that this is also the way they are behind closed doors with the business partners; it's not just a public display of fairness and caring for people. Some of us know a fake when we see one even if they try to pretend. As I watched these women respect all that came before them, I had a quick flash back to where we came from where the so-called leaders acted obnoxious, partial, egotistical, with an air of 'divide and conquer', manipulative, divisive, nepotistic, racist, 'clickly', and 'slicky'. OMG, what are the other words I could think of to describe how nasty they were? Their behaviors were unprofessional, unscrupulous, and even worse, unconscionable.

They literally wished they could eat their cake and have it too, meaning that they wished they could get you to bring your people, and after that you should disappear and give the stage and money solely to them. They gave credit to no one but themselves when they knew deep in their hearts that they could never have gotten there without your efforts and major contributions.

These PHPI leaders are the opposite, never in a hurry to get you off the phone and always very pleasant to speak with. Even if they have to go while you are on the phone with them, they will do it with dignity and respect, leaving you feeling like an equal. They really understand that when people are treated with respect, dignity and given their dues, they are at their best and they produce with ease, and it becomes a win-win for all. Isn't that what everyone is looking for everywhere they go?

No one flourishes in a negative or divisive environment. I know for a fact that conflict destroys concentration and productivity. So, I quickly remove myself from such an environment once it is clear that this is what that environment breeds and the people in charge just don't care until it is too late in the game.

This is the reason why Beth Henson Phillips, Betty Miles and Richard Pressley are exemplary leaders and people to emulate. I, along with many others, am a student under their tutelage and am sure that by the time I graduate, I will be better than my teachers.

In Ibo language, we often would say that "*onye ji nmadu na la, ji owe ya.*" That means when you hold someone down, you are holding yourself down as well, because for you to get up, you have to release the person you are holding down. If you don't want to get up, then continue to hold that individual down and both of you will get nowhere but remain down.

The reason for this Ibo proverb is that these honorable leaders I discussed here proved that the other leaders that I experienced in my previous company got it all wrong, because in their effort to block your blessings, they stifle their own blessings as well. Let me just give you an example of what I mean.

L-R: Beth Hinson Phillips. Margaret Dureke & President & CEO of PHPI Derrick Rodgers

In the company I came from previously, whenever there was an event or opportunity that the 'corporate' was converging to mingle with the field, the so-called leaders (who would not have been able to get to the top without you) would do everything to hide and keep others from being a part of it or from meeting the 'corporate.' They literally choked from thinking that you might meet the owners and be discovered as additional talent for the goodness of the company. The 'corporate' also did not do anything visible with the field on its own to make sure the field was unified, and at times it seemed like the 'corporate' perpetuated the conflicts and the idiosyncratic and unwarranted behaviors of the leadership with some of the corporate employees. I strongly believe this led to the massive exodus of representatives at some point.

So, they did everything to block any opportunity and would literally die rather than allow you to be a presenter of the opportunity because in their impoverished state of being, they thought that someone else was capable of taking their places. Eleanor Roosevelt stated many years ago that an inferiority complex is a state of mind and that "*no one can make you feel inferior without your permission or consent.*" These people were very insecure and poor in spirit. Beth, Betty and a whole lot of others in PHPI got it right. That is one of the reasons why PHPI will go down in the annals of network marketing history as the one that did what others wished to have done. I am really very happy to be a part of such an awesome group of professionals that believe in their people.

To make it in life or business, you have to have that **unstoppable force to be reckoned with** against the wishes of your enemies or those who do not wish you well.

L-R: Beth Henson Phillips, the FIRST documented First Lady of Network marketing & our mother at PHPI, Margaret Dureke, and the Queen of network marketing Betty Miles, who is the former First Lady of South Carolina and wife of the former Secretary of State of South Carolina who is also a Lawyer herself.

Contrasting the experience from my previous company to my experience with Beth Henson Phillips and Betty Miles – the latter is simply a class act. Here is what I mean: after I met the founder and CEO of PHPI, Beth went the extra mile to tell Mr. Rodgers a lot more about me and my work and what

I bring to the table of the company. I was like, what? It must be a new day.

When I asked Betty Miles to foreword this book, she thought of it as an honor for me to ask her to do it for me. That is how humble and respectful she is toward others. These leaders are very secure in themselves; they know who they are and are not worried and scared to death that you may succeed. So, they encourage their partners to succeed and not engage in the *divide and conquer spirit of most leaders* in the industry. And from all indication, they don't try to control the uncontrollable (human destiny) and delusional thinking that it is all about them.

How to Avoid the Damage Network Marketing Can Do to Your Life and Business

1. If you know what you want, you can have it! What is your 'why'?

One of the biggest game changers for those that make it in network marketing is often that they know their 'why' for getting involved and they stay the course to achieve it. Staying the course to achieve does not necessarily mean staying with the same company you started with even when it is no longer working for you. For me, change of process is not failure; it is a necessary ingredient for successful people. In other words, like in my situation, the idea that I can find a viable avenue in which I can earn money residually for years to come by just investing a nominal amount or a turnkey investment, meant that I had to keep my eye on the prize even if it meant changing a couple of vehicles to obtain my goals. That is exactly what I did, and today we have a home with PHPI. I did not allow my past to hold me hostage. Rather, it empowered me to *find creative ways* to succeed because the *best revenge in life is living well and succeeding.*

2. Be comfortable in your own skin

When you are comfortable in your own skin, it means you know who you are, where you came from and where you are going. When you know who you are and whose you are, no one can push you out of your position. When you are comfortable in your own skin, it means that you will not allow anyone to intimidate you or make you do what you have no business doing. When you are comfortable in your own skin, it means that you are no longer a people pleaser. It also means that **NOW** you know the difference between being nice and being stupid. You are confident in your own belief system and what you can do regardless of what others may think of you. Be mindful of the brain washing. It is your state of mind and your state of being. Protect it with every fiber of your being because the battle is won or lost in the brain.

3. Be sure of what it is you want in the first place before joining a network business

"If you know what you want, you can have it!"

The best way to discuss this is to refer back to the basic premise of one of my books, "How to Succeed Against All Odds," which is *"If you know what you want, you can have it!"* It is a lot harder to be knocked out of your game plan if you are convicted of your **'why'** that got you into the business. If from the jumpstart you know exactly what you want, no human being or challenge that you may encounter along the way will take you out of it until you find your new home. An example of someone who has demonstrated that he knows what he wanted is a legend in the industry and the second richest man in the world – Bill Gates. When he got convicted with a vision that with the Microsoft program someday every household in America would have a desktop computer and thereby need his software as an operating system, no amount of naysayers and challenges to the fact of that vision would be strong enough to stop him. Everyone by now knows how that story ended.

He is a man who has demonstrated time and again that if you know what you want and you are determined, creative, and become a prisoner of hope – proactively – and you are willing to sacrifice, *you can have it* (whatever the "it" may be for you).

4. Believe in yourself and your purpose!

The power of **belief** is the key to self-empowerment, and self-empowerment is equal to success – as I espoused profoundly in my bestseller, **How to Succeed against All Odds!** If you don't believe in yourself and in what you are marketing, no one else will. Remember, "Self help is the best help." Let others leave their futures in someone else's hands; not you. The belief here is 110% percent and not 99.9%, because for less than .01% doubt you are out or you achieve mediocrity. If you don't believe 110%, don't join, because you will not succeed. The best way to manage risk is to find a business and invest in a company that has very low risk – such as PHPI or other similar ones out there that I am not aware of that are good.

5. Be willing to sacrifice and work for what you want

Oftentimes many people want the best that the world has to offer, but the shocking thing is that they don't want to work or sacrifice anything for it. Yet they believe they deserve it. It is never going to happen this way, because in life and business you don't get what you want or deserve, but what you negotiate and make happen. We all know by now that "if wishes were horses, beggars would ride."

6. Never join to please someone else

One of the ways to avoid the damage that this business could do to you and your business is: you should never join solely to please someone else. If you join solely to please someone else or so that someone will not get mad at you, you will never make it because that is not a strong 'why'. *It means that you did not see the opportunity for yourself.* Those who make it in this business are those who see it for themselves and have strong enough **'why'** and are focused and determined to succeed. Some of the people, who join to please someone else, often will forget about the business they joined. They also often forget that they put their credit card into the system and over time, they are charged, and when they finally realize that the company has been billing them, they get very upset and begin to bad-mouth the company when in fact it is not the company's fault.

These become some of the people who bad-mouth the network marketing business without telling people the truth as to how they got to the bad experience. **Never** join just to please someone else.

7. Listen to everyone, but trust only yourself and a very small few

In network marketing, you will hear it all. People will come at you with all kinds of information. Some are self serving; others are objective in nature but flawed with bad motives behind what is being brought to you.

My advice is that you keep an open mind; listen to everyone, because you just never know what useful information may come out of it. However, make use of your own independent thinking and processing. In the end, make a decision based on your own accord, incorporating only what you believe and trusting a few of your close mastermind alliance group or mentors. Guard your mind and thoughts very closely lest you become very vulnerable to the shenanigans of others.

8. "To be independent of public opinion is the first formal condition of achieving anything great." – Georg Hegel

You must be independent of other peoples' opinions if you want to achieve anything great in life or business. A lot of people are often swayed in the wrong direction just because someone who may or may not know a thing or two about what they are about to do advises them to the contrary.

Most ordinary people just can't achieve beyond mediocrity just because they want to belong and be loved and accepted by others even when the association or opinion is not beneficial to them. I call this the 'people pleasing syndrome' which can also show up in people as a form of inferiority complex symptom.

So, believe in yourself and your course regardless of what the naysayers are going to say. Either way, they are going to talk about you. So, why not do what you planned on doing and use your life and success as a way to answer back.

How to Succeed in Network Marketing

1. **Even if you have "tried" network marketing (MLM) before and it did not work for you, you can still make it if you know how!**

Timing and positioning is everything in network marketing and positioning and action must happen before success can occur. The fact that the few times you attempted in the past did not work is not necessarily fatal, because I believe that *"failure is simply the opportunity to begin again but more intelligently."* – Henry Ford

I personally believe that the only time you fail is when you stop trying. Why don't you fail your way to success like Thomas Edison did when he discovered electricity that we all enjoy today!

2. Using People Helping People (PHPI) as a case study and a case in point!

I think that the best way to demonstrate how to succeed in the network marketing business if you have already made up your mind that it is the right avenue for you and your family to earn more as "plan B", or the only way to earn financial freedom, is to demonstrate with a company that models and contains all the components and tenets of a good opportunity with the company for all intents and purposes.

People Helping People, Inc. (PHPI) a case study and a case in point!

Meet the president of People Helping People, Inc. (PHPI), Mr. Derrick Rodgers.

Mr. Rodgers is a man who has no qualms about acknowledging that God is the true source of all of his successes and that he is nobody without God! He is a man who truly believes that all people can be helped, no matter where they may live on the face of the earth, by simply taking the first step to help one person, and that one helps the next one and so forth. Paying it forward is Mr. Rodgers' biggest thing. He believes that we are here to give and pay it forward and has even said to the field that we should be known as the company of givers – something I have never heard before in corporate America. His business methodology is based on this premise, which is contrary to Wall

Street and Corporate Americas' business mindset that overtly or covertly preaches greed and grab all you can no matter whose lives are ruined as a result. This approach is simply a breath of fresh air in the marketplace.

This company is the latest "babe" in town – **People Helping People, Inc. (PHPI)**. Before I begin to tell you why PHPI is the right company to use as a model, let me tell you up front that I am involved with this company, and I am one of its business partners and one of the founding members.

By the time you get through reading this book, you will understand why, and I am convinced that you will have your aha! moment. What I am sure you will agree with so far is that you don't just get and begin to write a book of this magnitude from going through nothing. I have often said in my speaking platforms that you cannot minister where you have not bled. I have been to the top of a network marketing company that was not what it was cracked up to be, but what I learned is invaluable, and I would not trade the experience for anything. It rather prepared the ground for me to know that the industry is buzzing with trillions of dollars and to know how to decipher what to look for in a company that will give me and my family the dividend of everlasting generational passive residual income even when we walk away from it.

The "new Babe" in town – PHPI

Now that I have set the stage for you, let's go back to this "new babe" in town (PHPI) that will go down in the annals of history for its unique compensation plan and business approach – human beings' first approach since the history of MLM or the direct sales industry.

After I outlined this section, I was thinking about the best way to start it when the owner of PHPI, Derrick Rodgers, guest-starred on our regular Friday leadership call, and lo and behold, he opens the curtain the best way for this segment of the book. Then, I was in the process of transcribing as much as

I could from Mr. Rodgers' speech to us, when I received a very well-transcribed version from one of the leaders of the company. So, I thanked the good Lord for the perfect timing (<u>timing </u>and <u>positioning</u> at its best) and decided to use it. Here it is, and I will explain why below:

<u>YOUR MILLION DOLLAR INTERVIEW</u>!

Imagine for a minute you just took out a small business loan for $1 Million Dollars to start your own business. Really...you just signed the promissory note and you are going to have to pay the bank back $1 million...with interest! (Kind of a scary thought for some of us, right?)

Okay – your first task as a new business owner is to hire your COO – Chief Operations Officer. This is the person who will be in charge of the day-to-day operations of your new business.

Basically...this is your new business partner and if they fail in their position...it could cost you $1 million dollars out of your pocket!!!

Do you think you would pick and choose your partner VERY CAREFULLY?

Would you design a very detailed interview to make sure they were right for the job?

Would you want to get to know as much about them as possible?

Would you want to know the plans, philosophies and strategies they plan to implement for the success of your business?

Would you want to know who they plan on using for outside vendors and why?

(Maybe you would want to meet them also)

Would you want to know their commitment and dedication levels?

Would you want to know if they were truly honest and trustworthy?

Would you want to know if they had irreproachable integrity and unquestionable character?

Basically – wouldn't you want to know their heart?

Folks, many of you are considering choosing People Helping People, Inc. to be YOUR business partner – PHPI will be in charge of many of the aspects of your business – from vendors to philosophies to strategies to compensation and much, much more! Don't you want to know the answers to the questions above as it relates to your business???

The absolute BEST WAY to determine if PHPI is the best business partner you could choose to secure your fortune...is to interview them. And guess what??? In only 2 weeks...that's 14 days from today...YOU will get YOUR CHANCE to get those – and many more – questions answered...in RALEIGH, NC!

I believe PHPI really wants the job as YOUR business partner because they are pulling out all the stops! They have reserved the space for you to interview beginning at 8pm EST at the Raleigh Convention Center on Friday, May 14th. They want to make sure you are in a great mindset to listen to their presentation of why they should get the job, so they are throwing a gala bash for you to get things rolling. They will have live music, great food, refreshing beverages…and, they will have some special guests there with some special announcements for YOU!

Then, they will spend the entire day Saturday laying out the answers to all the questions you could have…and more! They even have some surprises for you to really make you know and believe in your heart that they are the right ones for you and will get the job done!

They are going to let you meet and greet the vendors they have chosen to align with to make your business the best it could possibly be! There will even be specialized coaching sessions on the various services and products your new business venture will be able to offer.

I've even heard they are going to have products and services available for you to leave there with that are customized and branded to your new business so you can show others you made the right choice!

They are even going to invite you to attend a Christian Worship Service on Sunday so you can know where their heart is and who they give the glory to! – (Bud Nemeth's transcription of Mr. Rodgers' interview)

Margaret Dureke and Mr. Derrick Rodgers during their private conversation and time together.

I was attentive to every word he shared with me because I know that when those who have been where you are going speak, you pay attention and take in as much information as you can, because I know that his time and expertise are precious and valuable. I was grateful that he was willing to share with me. I was also eager to pick up as many clues as possible – as we all now know, successful people leave clues.

Based on my research and information, what Mr. Rodgers said that is the criteria we use when we are out there recruiting a potential business partner, is historic. It has not been done before. I have heard a variation of it before but never from the perspective from which he shared it.

My spiritual alignment with that of our able President and CEO Derrick Rodgers is something out of a science fiction movie. For a long time, I struggled with companies, people, and organizations that would ask or want me to separate my spiritual beliefs from my speeches and presentations. Even though I always said 'yes' to them, when it came down to it, I always ended up spilling my spirituality into my speech – not because I wanted to disobey them, but because like Mr. Rodgers says, "how do you separate your spirit from your work?" Your work is synonymous and tantamount to your spirit, and to separate one from the other is to live a lie and to speak a lie.

I was really blown away when Mr. Rodgers told me during my private conversation with him that without God, he is nothing. It was not because he said it that blew me away, but that I felt the heart and sincerity with which he said it and the thought that for the first time, I am in business with a wealthy man that is non-apologetic about who he credits for his successes and being.

I shared my major defining moment in my Christian belief test with Mr. Rodgers, and again he rose to the occasion and even referred me to a Bible verse for the answer to that.

I went on to share with Mr. Rodgers how I got a test of monumental proportions a few years back when a purchaser for major personal development books for a major corporation propositioned me with an offer that was very irresistible. This person loved my books but said that the only way they would buy my books as they proposed buying them in several hundreds of thousands of copies, would be for me to reprint the books and take God out anywhere there was a reference to God in my books.

Wow! What do you do with this kind of offer? Sell your soul and make money – or keep your soul and gain peace despite the need and desire to sell the books at such magnitude, because you really need the money?

Before I could even tell him that I did not do it, Mr. Rodgers said "don't do it." He then pointed me to the scripture book of *Jeremiah 1* and encouraged me to go back and read it, saying that I would understand why I should not do it. I then told him that even though it was a very difficult decision at the time, I did not do it and I did not regret it, because God has been very kind to me and still shows me favor daily.

I quickly made a mental note of his advice to read the book of *Jeremiah 1* and what it has to say about the subject we had discussed. I got excited when he said that because I know that successful people leave clues of their success steps, and I knew immediately that the information Mr. Rodgers just shared with me was a big drop for my use.

I quickly went to grab a Bible and went straight to the book of Jeremiah, the first chapter. I quickly and intently read the first book of *Jeremiah*. After I read it, I got what Mr. Rodgers was alluding to when he referred me to it. My faith again grew deeper than it was prior to my conversation with Mr. Rodgers. It was not that I was not familiar with the book of Jeremiah. I just could not recall exactly what it said pertaining to the subject we had discussed. Upon reading it, I got the message and see why Mr. Rodgers referred me to it.

Here are a few verses that stuck out to me immediately: *verses 5, 8, and 19.* The whole chapter was relevant, but these verses spoke directly to the issue of not being afraid and realizing that the God we serve had prepared my path before I was born and that I should not be afraid of them and their faces. You can read it for yourself to get the whole gist of what *Jeremiah 1* is about and how you can gain your own insight, inspiration and introspection from it.

3. Treat your business as your million dollar business and not as a hobby!

After reading these criteria as transcribed by Bud Nemeth, it becomes apparent that Mr. Rodgers understands – as I believe – that the number one reason most people in network marketing don't make it is that they treat it as a hobby and not as a serious business. Just as was expressed by the founder and owner of People Helping People, Inc. (PHPI), what if **you** had to be the one to put up the millions of dollars that starting these types of businesses requires? Would you hire you or treat it shabbily?

Network marketing: A concept worth defending!

I think it is pertinent to start this section with some of what the experts are saying about the industry:

(a) Warren Buffet: "The best investment I ever made....," regarding the network marketing companies he purchased, one of which was "The Pampered Chef".

(b) "Network marketers are creating fortunes at breakneck speed." – *Success Magazine*

(c) "Network Marketing: the perfect business for the average person to create wealth." – Robert Kiyosaki (author of *Poor Dad, Rich Dad*).

(d) "Network marketing is the best-kept secret in the business world." – *Fortune Magazine*

Margaret Dureke defended network marketing in *The Washington Post Magazine*

In an article that was published in *The Washington Post Magazine* of Sunday July 9, 2009 entitled: "THE FINANCE ISSUE: Point of Sale: Pyramid businesses are booming in Prince George's County during the recession" (*Margaret Dureke was quoted for defending network marketing*).

"Just not for everyone," as I was quoted for defending network marketing in order to help you understand why I defended it and still do and to distinguish the *Post* article with what I know to be true in the industry with respect to why some make it and others don't; and as to why it is not much different than what happens in corporate America or in most global marketplaces in the world.

4. Dare to dream and hope again!

"Success is not final; failure is not fatal; it is the courage to continue that matters." – Winston Churchill

To dream is to be alive, and not to dream is to be dead. To dream and act is to succeed, and to dream and do nothing about it is to fail. The only time you fail is when you quit "trying". If my husband and I did not keep the faith and continue to "try", we would have missed the opportunity to become today a founding member of PHPI. Because we know for a fact that there is no power in quitting, we stayed the course in the face of all the challenges and the seemingly impossible odds until God made a way and brought us home to PHPI.

You don't give up just because you've had a negative past. Until you get the monkey off your back, you can't settle, give up and complain.

5. The Five-Tier Factorial Litmus Test

*The **five-tier factorial litmus test** you must conduct when deciding whether a particular network marketing business opportunity is for you – **"if it does not fit, you must acquit."*** – Johnnie Cochran

A. Timing and Positioning!

In the real estate industry it's called, "location, location, location." In network marketing it is called, "timing and positioning, timing and positioning, and timing and positioning."

"Positioning and action must come before success. The man who comes up with a means for doing or producing almost anything better, faster or more economically has his future and his fortune at his fingertips." – *J. Paul Getty*

Start or position yourselves in front of an upcoming product/service (trend/shift) in the marketplace that has the capability to expand and not become stale. *Look for products and services that are not fads that will not fade with time, like telecommunication for an example.* This gives that business individual a unique advantage that most people without good business acumen or vision would not have (in other words, take a calculated risk). Don't wait until the idea becomes popular, because by that time the opportunity is gone! What most people don't understand is that when they get disappointed because a prospect did not see the opportunity because of its newness, is that if everyone saw it, then it's no longer an opportunity. When it becomes popular, it is no longer an opportunity. "No one can possibly achieve any real and lasting success or 'get rich' in business by being a conformist." – *J. Paul Getty*

B. Products and services with Universal Appeal that everyone <u>needs</u> and not <u>wants</u>!

Make sure that the product and/or service has universal or global appeal, whereby almost every race, age group, sex, size of pocket book or nationality <u>needs</u> it and not <u>wants</u> it. Sometimes, if you have the vision, it can even start locally, then nationally and finally internationally. It must be something that everyone needs even if they cannot afford it.

C. Business module must have leveraging capability to it, using a simple system (ease of duplication)!

This system must ensure that even in your absence the business goes on and is not solely dependent on your efforts alone. This fact is essential if you truly want to build wealth in your business and not just be LABORING day in and day out without much improvement/profit (leverage in the marketplace). If you want to experience exponential growth that comes from a business that allows the owner to leverage, you must stay away from business opportunities/ employment that do the following:

(a) **Exchange of Time for Money**. The danger here is when you are not working/laboring, you are not making money – your money is not working for you, but rather you are working for your money. Here, you are LABORING and not LEVERAGING. (Statistics show that 95% of the world's populations earn a living this way.) This way of earning and living is called "linear" earning and in leveraging it is called "residual" or passive income.

(b) **Exchange your EXPERTISE and knowledge/education for money!** This means that the expert's earnings are only limited to the amount of time he/she trades for money. The problem here again is that it is often good while it lasts, but at some point in one's life, the reality of solo journey to financial freedom is not the answer. This is because you cannot build wealth by yourself. Also, when the professional, for example a Medical Doctor, is not performing, he or she is not making any money, and this will often not translate to generational wealth. What if he falls sick? – God forbid – but what happens?

(c) **Sole Proprietor/CEO (Me-Myself-and-I, Inc.) business ownership!** This type of business model is the worst and most intensive of them all. Everything centers on "me-myself-and-I", 24/7, 365 days a year, and then every year things remain the same or get worse in some instances. You may be able to pay your bills and all, but you will NEVER BUILD TRUE WEALTH THAT IS BIGGER THAN LIFE AND YOU UNLESS – YOUR BUSINESS INCORPORATES THE LIFE-CHANGING CONCEPT OF LEVERAGING AS ESPOUSED BY THE FIRST DOCUMENTED BILLIONAIRE IN AMERICA, J. PAUL GETTY:

J. Paul Getty said, *"I would rather earn 1% off a 100 people's efforts than 100% of my own efforts."* This implies that if he gets sick and he is being paid on 100% of his own efforts, then his income goes to 0. However, if he is getting paid 1% each on the efforts of 100 people, if one of them gets sick, he still gets 99%.

If you stay with the "me-myself-and-I" mindset as a business person, in time you will be depleted of all your resources and soon break down and fold as many do. The same is true for those individuals who hold 9-5 jobs that run 2-3 shifts on end with the mindset that the more hours or jobs they hold, the more money they are going to make. That is also an illusion in the long run. Two jobs are meant for two people and at times prove to be unhealthy for just one individual and his/her family. This is still not the answer, and the truth is that they still can't make ends meet at the end of the day with the different shifts and jobs that they hold. In the long run, they are slowly but surely killing themselves with that lifestyle unbeknownst to some of them.

However, by leveraging the talents/efforts of others, employing others and/or opening many affiliates like Sam Walton, J. Paul Getty, Warren Buffet, Bill Gates, Donald Trump and many more did, you leverage your fortune! Wealth is created mainly by either having people work for you by way of leveraging/duplication/affiliates or having money at work for you by way of investment and reinvestment. Let's face it, no matter how hard you work (Me-Myself-and-I, Inc.), you can never create wealth sitting in one place from 9-5 and without duplication. **The answer again is LEVERAGING!** It is not the intensity of the LABOR that builds wealth; rather it is in how smart you get to leverage the opportunities you come across. One of the greatest advantages of leveraging in the network marketing industry is that everyone has the opportunity to start from the same level and platform and it does not discriminate – anyone can do it as long as they are coach-able and teachable!

D. AFFORDABLE/EASE OF ENTRY

Affordable or ease of entry simply means a turnkey investment amount that the average person out there can afford. 'Affordable' means a nominal fee, as in the case of PHPI that charges only a minimum fee of $49.99 or $99.99 to start the business.

E. PRODUCT MUST SELL ITSELF –As Network Marketing Legend Bernard McCargo puts it.

This means products and services that sell themselves – those that have universal appeal without you trying to *convince* anyone as to why they need to buy the products and services like we have in PHPI. Everyone is already consuming most of PHPI's products and services. PHPI is only showing people how they can save money and make money from what they are already using. It must be a need and not a want. It goes without saying that the telecommunication business is recession proof, and if the service plan makes money sense and savings sense, the customer does not need anyone to hammer him or her over the head to want it – just like we have with PHPI. Unlike our competition, we offer a prepaid, unlimited calling plan with all the bells and whistles – no contract, no credit check, no additional usage charges and taxes added to the inexpensive plan. We offer no post-paid contract or credit check pressures like our competitors do.

In presenting the PHPI opportunity, some people's quick and immediate response is usually – "this other wireless company is already doing that." My next question/comment to them is, "How much are you getting back from that other wireless company every month when you pay your phone bill?" The next thing they say almost all the time in response is, "Oh, I never thought about it like that." Then from there, the rest is history.

It's really an exciting time to be alive! We all know by now that what is happening globally today is a **MAJOR SHIFT** in wealth trend in the marketplace and in the telecommunication industry specifically. It is only those who dare to take "the road less traveled," go where others would not go and position themselves at the right time, with the right products, the right company and services, the right opportunity and the right people, who will emerge as **winners** in the **next generational wealth shift** starting right NOW! IT IS A DECADE OF RESTORATION AND COMPLETION. DON'T LET YOURS PASS YOU BY! Stop singing recession and start finding creative ways to position yourself in front of the next major shift in wealth going on right now.

F. Compensation plan that offers walk-away residual income ("mailbox money")

I have been around three telecom network marketing companies and observed their compensation plans, and I can honestly and unequivocally tell you that again PHPI has passed the test with flying colors for a true network marketing company that has the capability and the heart to give someone a real walk-away income and generational wealth. How do I know this if the company is new? That is a fair and good question, because when someone has a personal stake in a company they are positively projecting, bias can easily slip in. So, here is how I know. Like I often would say, "you cannot minister where you have not bled; I have tasted and I have seen." For the very first month, residual income we earned from PHPI for just one short month is larger than our residual income from the companies we were with previously. Yes, with those companies you make immediate quick money up front, but the residual income, which was my main reason for getting involved, was nothing to write home about.

"To reach a port, you must sail, sail, not tie at the anchor, sail not drift." – *Franklin Roosevelt*

I believe that the worst chance to take is the one you did not take. The fact that the few times you "tried" you did not get the desired result does not mean that you are now out of the running. "He who fights and runs away will live to fight another day." – Bob Marley. The big elephant of not having enough and being financially free has not yet left your dining table. So, quitting or not doing anything about your current state is not an option.

I believe that you stick and stay until you get your pay – not necessarily with the first or even second vehicle you started with. So, you don't quit on your objective, but you can quit on the method or vehicle of operation and go again until you find your post or home. There is a post or home for everyone; find your own. Do something **Now** and not tomorrow because procrastination and excuses are the thieves of time. It is all about your mindset and thought process.

6. My recommendations

Take a chance and position yourself (What if this could be the one?) – regardless of your past experiences.

If you don't take a chance and position yourself in front of the opportunity in the first place, this book will have no meaning for you except that you are reading it just to be informed because *the power of knowledge is not embedded in its acquisition, but in its application.* Unlike many people, I don't just read to be informed. I read to be empowered to take action. I know for a fact that information is not power unless it is put to use.

In a forwarded email from Betty Miles, she said:
"*I've spent the last 15 years experiencing the incredible benefits of this industry, and I've shared it with as many people as I could! I've seen the most unlikely people become millionaires, and many of the most deserving of success, fall short of the desired income, in spite of tireless effort and hard work.*"

Again, I repeat that successful people leave clues. So, it is pertinent to listen and copy people like Ms. Miles and step out in faith regardless of how different and uncomfortable it may seem initially. To be comfortable, it often requires that you first become uncomfortable. I have come to realize and understand that it is only those in motion that God propels to the next level because they are not just hearing the word, they are doing the word. What if this is the one? How would you know if you did not give it a 'try' or chance? No one grows without taking chances or stepping outside their comfort zone. If you go down the memory lane of the journeys of successful entrepreneurs, you will learn that it is mainly those who dared to venture where others would say, "not for me" that were able to achieve that which seemed impossible. They have always aspired to achieve that which is impossible like Bill Gates. Network marketing, which incorporates multi-level marketing, often avails a significant amount of people the opportunity to leverage their efforts and talents like no other place in the marketplace.

So, what is **leveraging** and why should you care?

To understand and appreciate the power of leveraging, you remember what J. Paul Getty, the first documented billionaire in America, said: *"I would rather earn 1% off a 100 people's efforts than 100% of my own efforts."*

The key here is LEVERAGING AND NOT LABORING. The distinction between the two is that leveraging involves duplication, system, uniformity, simplicity, continuity, while laboring requires *singularity of intense effort by an individual.* We all know by now that no one can build wealth singularly. Wealthy people leverage and ordinary people labor.

A quick overview of the successful business moguls like J. Paul Getty, Warren Buffet, and Sam Walton, just to mention a few, will elucidate the point here as we all know by examining the footsteps of these successful individuals' lives and the clues they left behind!

Be mindful that those who focus on the "recession" will miss what time it is. It is time to get very creative and roll up your sleeves and let your imagination go 'berserk'. Remember that whatever you focus on will expand and vice versa. If you think you can, then you can; the "can'ts" cannot be where the "cans" are. Don't just become comfortably miserable and think that "this is it" because it is not, and it's never too late to start anew. *Don't forget your pockets of power – to reach deep down in your soul for it and equip yourself and go again.* If you did it before, you can do it again. If you have never done it and have been sitting on the fence, it is time to get off the fence, because we all know what happens to fence sitters – they get shot both ways!

Are you sick and tired of being sick and tired? If your answer is yes, what are you going to do about it? You realize that to have what you have never had, you have to be willing to do what you have never done! To get through, you must be willing to go through, because there is no other way and no one escapes from the school of life. The moment you are willing to go through, then you will get through. If you are not willing, you will remain in the wilderness and complain – and because you complain, you remain.

The good news is that there is something out there for everyone; you just have to continue to search until you find it, because it does not come to you in a vacuum. Remember that if you pursue that which is impossible, then you achieve that which is possible; and if you pursue that which is possible, then you achieve mediocrity. The actions or non-actions we take today will determine the quality of our future. So, start today to walk toward the mark!

Don't feel overwhelmed or stymied about it all, because the ONLY way to eat an elephant is one bite at a time and realize that the minute you take that first bite – no matter how small the bite is – it is no longer a whole elephant. *That should be your mindset going into anything you want but don't know how or where to start – **Just go for it**.* Don't get into too much analysis that at some point may cause you to be paralyzed with the analysis and soon become what they call a victim of "paralysis of analysis." Take action and go for it if it makes sense that there may be something there for you. What if it doesn't turn out to be what you thought it was going to be? So what? Your life did not get any worse than it was as many people seem to think when the journeys turn out contrary to what they originally had in mind. As I heard someone say, "If it is not God sent, it will be God used." So, step out in faith and see what lies around the corner for you! **YES, you can!**

~In life and business, you don't get what you want or deserve, but what you negotiate and make happen!~

No "isms" at least in the beginning and up to a certain point.

Like any other place where people gather, at some point, human nature will set in and people will begin to make choices of who they prefer to have in their teams, socialize with and for whom they want to do favors. I saw this happen first hand in one of the previous companies I was involved with for some time. My finding was that the company owners start favoritism – favoring some people and disregarding the hard work and efforts of the others. Sometimes, they say they do it to encourage competition. I know that it does not work for long, because it often leads to obnoxious and rude behaviors by those that are favored and resentment by those that are disregarded, ignored, neglected, and isolated.

The mistake that the owners of the business make is that they forget that everyone who joins network marketing is not particularly hungry. Some join for various reasons and cannot and would not allow anyone to tread upon their integrity and humility.

~In life and business, you don't get what you want or deserve, but what you <u>negotiate</u> and <u>make happen</u>!~

When you encounter this in your network, you don't quit the ideal or knowledge of what network marketing can do for you. Rather, you change the vehicle and still make it happen for you and your family.

Network marketing offers a level playing field to all who are interested regardless of one's background, race, gender, religion or any of those discriminatory mind games that take place in the marketplace/ corporate America or other places for that matter that often lead a lot of people to feel less than half of a human being.

Network marketing allows everyone an equal opportunity to get involved and take a chance-of-a- lifetime opportunity that they would not otherwise have. They don't have to show that they are either over-qualified which disqualifies them, or under- qualified which again makes them not employable. You come as you are. And because your promotion in most instances is determined by the system and not by another human being – a practice that most of the time is so biased against you and is more prone to be mentally or emotionally or psychologically demeaning – with network marketing, when you find the right one for you, it can in fact show you that you have more power and worth in life than you ever thought you had.

The upward mobility that you can get from being involved with network marketing and the personal development that you will gain as a result of being a network marketing agent, often as far as I am concerned totally outweighs any negative. Like any other business, it of course has its ups and its downs. However, I believe that if you know who you are, what you want and what you bring to the table, it can be one of the best things that ever happened to you wholistically.

It is established now that there is no industry that does not have the possibility of a scam artist in it. Therefore, this should not be anything that is singled out regarding network marketers. So, we are going to keep things in their proper perspective in order to see the truth about the industry so that those who care to take advantage of network marketing to change their families' financial lives can freely do so. Especially today when most are hurting financially, network marketing can be the difference in your living the American Dream. It does not cost much to get involved in most cases, like in PHPI, and you don't have to be educated to be successful in it. My finding is that most educated people do not do well in these businesses because they are busy trying to figure out what is wrong with the process. It seems that the less educated individuals go in innocently, without a lot of presumptions and egos and often find that it changes their families' lives.

Network marketing, in fact, allows the small man to own his or her own business for very little money – a business that he or she would not have otherwise been able to afford. The way financing is structured in corporate America, if you are a small man in business, it would be easier for you to go to hell and get financing successfully than try the so-called financial institutions that are supposed to be there for you – unless, of course, you have a godfather in Abraham. This fact deters a lot of would-be entrepreneurs from venturing out in the first place.

So, they do nothing but take a 9-5 job and procrastinate on launching out until it's too late to take a chance on their dreams, and hence they become bitter and angry at the system. This is not to say that everyone who has a 9-5 job wants to own their business or are not happy with it. So, get over that, because that is not what the subject matter is about here. It is about those who say to the contrary. This is where network marketing allows the "big boys" who have the money to take the necessary steps and put all the protocols in place for starting and succeeding in a home-based business. Then the small guys step in and pay their minimal fees which we call a "turn-key investment fee" and get a chance to own home-based businesses, the freedom to do what they want and when they want and much more."

Network marketing is one marketplace in which an individual can be catapulted from zero to zillion just because he or she took a chance for a nominal fee that they otherwise could not have been able to afford on their own. I don't know anywhere else or any other opportunities out there that can avail ordinary people such extraordinary opportunities to change their financial well-being and keep hope alive at the same time. This is part of what makes America the greatest country in the world where anyone, regardless of what their last name is or isn't, can make it if they know how to persevere to learn the ropes of success and stay the course to achieve.

Getting involved in network marketing can open the door to other means and ways of earning an honest and earnest living that you would not have known existed before. Network marketing can also get you into the corridors of power you would have not otherwise been invited into. Hence, it is an equal opportunity employer compared to any other industry out there.

~In life and business, you don't get what you want or deserve, but what you _negotiate_ and _make happen_!~

According to Jack Canfield, the author of *Chicken Soup for the Soul*, the three things that determine success are:

A. Mindset
B. Skill set
C. Environment

Which of the three are you lacking? Figure it out and fix it; that might be the bridge you need to cross over.

7. Be a supportive coach and not a manager

Build your team with the intention of helping everyone succeed.

Here are the cornerstones that any team must have to succeed:

9 Building Blocks any t-e-a-m (together everyone achieves more) must have in order to succeed:

   a. Clear and precise goal

   b. Results-driven objectives

   c. Completion NOT competition

   d. Collaborative effort - not individualized

   e. Committed and cooperative

   f. Meeting of the minds

   g. Not about one person or a select few

   h. No preferential treatment

   i. Do unto others as you wish them to do unto you.

*Some of my PHPI mastermind founding member
leadership team at the May 14-15, 2010 Pre-Launch
in Charlotte North Carolina.*

8. Bring out the best in your team

The way you treat people is the hallmark of how you
will end up in the long term in network marketing.
Help your team to grow in a very supportive and
constructive way so they will contribute more and
feel better about themselves. When they commit
more, the business grows for everyone. Together and

cooperatively we all achieve more and find greater satisfaction and fulfillment in working together.

9. 9 essential tools for successful team work

- Listen

- Understand

- Question

- Support

- Persuade

- Respect

- Share

- Help

- Participate

10. Build according to some rules of engagement of "Dos" and "Don'ts"

Here are your 13 "Dos" to building a successful team!

- Build up your team – no 'divide and conquer' that a lot of leaders practice that comes back over time to haunt and stifle the growth of their businesses.

- Lead by example. Do not be many things to many people to the extent that people don't even know what you believe in or stand for anymore. I believe that if you stand on the bench of integrity which may not be popular and build steadily, with time you will build for the long haul and grow exponentially, and no one can stop it, even if they wanted to. God will show up and show off on your behalf. God has done it for me time and again, and I am sure that He will do it for you too, because I know for a fact that God is no respecter of persons; what He does for one, He will do for another if you stand firm on the conditions of that promise.

- Listen to your team.

- Praise your team.

- Don't get ahead of yourself – always remember who got you there in the first place, because "ingratitude is base, and ungrateful people end badly."

- Socialize with your team – occasionally – with defined boundaries (expressed or implied).

- Make your network group feel very important and valued.

- Network – Attend social events to spread the vision with others.

- Keep an open mind, not a closed mind and opinions.

- Allow other emerging leaders to lead their leaders.

- Share your resources.

- Share personal development stories, strategies and materials.

- Keep a humble spirit and attitude.

Here are 10 "Don'ts" to building a successful network!

▪ Don't take things personally – though it's very hard not to do.

▪ Don't let others shift your confidence and focus.

▪ Don't allow friendship to affect your business.

▪ Don't turn your business into a social club.

▪ Don't make excuses – make money.

- Don't entertain gossip.

- Don't get too arrogant.

- Don't look down on others.

- Don't allow others to bring you down to their level. Look for and associate only with those who will elevate and encourage you to grow.

- **Build the best alliance on the block...**

  o Always chart the course for your organization.

  o Always be on your best behavior.

  o Always look your best.

  o Always expect the best from your team – when you sincerely praise them, you get the best from them.

11. Donald Trump and Network Marketing

It has been established that successful people leave clues. Therefore, it would make sense to refer to someone who is very successful in business and who has embraced the idea of network marketing and started his own businesses. That person is none other than Donald J. Trump. Everyone, except those who might be living in caves, know that Donald Trump made his money from real estate, and yet he has successfully endeavored to take advantage of many new marketing trends to further expand his financial empire. You would think that Donald Trump should be satisfied with what he has and do nothing more. That is often the mindset of most mediocre people. That is not Donald Trump. Mr. Trump wants it all, and there is nothing wrong with that because in a capitalist state, it is a free enterprise, and those who can, go for it. Today Donald Trump has his own network marketing company called Donald Trump Network.

Here is what Mr. Trump said: "You have to be smart and plan for your future. You can't expect your job or your government to create your wealth." Since we have already established that successful people leave clues, suffice it to say that the clue one should get from the above statement from Donald Trump could be summarized as follows:

A. If Donald Trump got into network marketing big time, why should regular employees discard the industry simply because they only make a few thousand dollars a year? I have often stated that if you know how much money you have in your bank account, you are not even rich – not to talk about being wealthy because wealth building is beyond having money alone.

B. People should keep an open mind at all times; the thing you dismissed might be the thing that could have taken you to your financial destiny. It is easy to see that Donald Trump is a very open-minded individual and that is part of why he is successful.

C. That if Donald Trump is in it, there is something there and it may be worth taking a first, second, third or even endless look at the opportunities to leverage. The reason I say this is that my finding is that a lot of people dismiss network marketing simply because they "tried" once before, and it did not work out for whatever reason. And ever since then they simply labeled it, "oh, one of those things that doesn't work," or "oh, those things are scams," or "it's only those who first started who will make money," etc. What people forget is that money never finishes. You can create wealth anytime, anywhere, like Carlos Slim, who is from Mexico and is the richest man in the world today, has proven. *Mr. Slim comes in at $53.5 billion, beating Microsoft founder Bill Gates to top the list of the world's richest people, according to a new ranking published by* <u>*Forbes*</u> *magazine.* You just have to have the right mindset and position yourself and be willing to go through to get through.

D. It also tells me that those who should be forcing to do the business are not, and those who should not, are – it is mind-boggling that that is the way it is. That is the reason why only 3% of the people in the world control the wealth.

E. Last but not least, you should ask yourself – If someone of the caliber of Donald Trump is doing network marketing and you are not, why? Warren Buffet, the third richest man in the world said that network marketing is the best investment he ever made in an interview he gave some time ago.

12. Let no one tamper with your sense of self and what you believe

If you come into network marketing without first having a strict sense of who you are along with strong self esteem, I can guarantee you that you will not make it. That is unless, of course, you are a diehard who is willing to go through to get through;

and this is very rare to find today in the marketplace. I recall what one of my business partners told me one day when she was questioning whether she would succeed in it. This made me think again about whether some people are better cut out for it than others.

This person told me that when she approached a certain individual to 'prospect' him about the business opportunity, the prospect told her that she had better stay with her 9-5 job, that she does not have what it takes, and that she would never make it. When my business partner told him that I am in the business and doing very well at it, he told her that he could see me doing very well at it, but not her. In fact, he proceeded to tell my business partner that he would be surprised if I was not one of the best at it.

Words could not begin to express how devastating my business partner was by that statement. She never really recovered from that blockbuster that the prospect gave to her self-esteem and confidence – even though I worked very hard to *resuscitate* her, to put life back into her, and to tell her to use the incident as a tool to go where she has never gone before. It is within her to prove to this prospect and herself that she can make it and that she is better and more capable than what the prospect thought of her.

Even though this partner told me that she was going to do exactly that, I can tell you that she never recovered from it no matter what I said and how much I tried to turn it around. Shortly thereafter, she started making excuses and finding reasons not to do what she needed to do to continue to build her business. At one point she confided in me and told me that since the negative encounter with the prospect, she found it very difficult to approach people to tell them about her business because every time she made an attempt, the negative statement that prospect told her rushed right into her mind and she would freeze.

Now, it produced a sense of worthlessness, and 'I can't do' attitudes. Like most people, after a few months of struggle, she finally caved in and quit the business. This situation is not peculiar to this individual alone in this industry. Also, soon after quitting their network marketing business, this category of people, when their friends and families ask them 'why', instead of telling the truth, they often tell them, "that thing does not work." These people I call, *"those who quit because they could not explain the business to their prospects and those who allow the "dream killers" to steal their dreams."* They have failed because they allowed someone else's thought process and mentality to affect and overpower theirs. It's sad, but true.

Here is what people don't understand: network marketing is one place that you get **FREE personal development training if you have the stamina to hold on.** You will be taken out of your comfort zone, and you will learn a lot about yourself and others out there whom, in many cases, you may not care for. However, that does not matter, because that is why it is called 'business' not 'social club'. It is simply war, and the only way you will win that war is if you are impeccably prepared for battle and you oil your mind and tools for success. You must also have an advancement at all cost mentality and not retract and recede just because some "Mr. or Mrs. or Ms. Spooky" individual who does not have his life in order tells you that you can't do it and you believe it.

Personally, negativism fuels and motivates me. What some people don't know is that nobody really gets up one day and becomes very strong. All you need to do is **make a decision** that life will not get the best of you no matter what life throws at you or what you bring into it yourself. You make the decision to get involved with life to the best of your ability and that you will NEVER GIVE UP no matter what. You also decide that NO human being has the power to destroy you unless you permit it – consciously or unconsciously.

This mindset is what separates those who go through and make it and those who go through and go down with it. This mindset is what distinguishes the winners from the losers. This mindset is what separates the failures and those who are successful –

and not necessarily because those that rose back from the setbacks or ashes of their lives are stronger or smarter – *they are simply stubborn against the odds of life.* This last statement is often what I answer to people who ask me time and again what my secret is! Those that make it know how to persevere and persist to get a breakthrough because they know that persistence will break resistance; and others who fail, don't.

I am by no means saying that everyone is the same, but I am saying that everyone has the potential to develop and become better than they were created or whatever way they find themselves or whatever circumstances in which they may find themselves.

Because of my involvement with network marketing, I have become stronger and more empowered than I was before starting. I have learned much more about the marketplace and the people in it and how you can't trust some of the people in it. This again does not mean that the industry is bad, but all people are greedy and would do anything to demean others in order to get ahead – **if YOU allow it!**

It is okay to be beaten once, but it is not okay to be beaten twice. You don't quit; you re-strategize and change your game plan. What I also find in this business is that most people quit once they are beaten the first time; some dare to go again, and on the second strike they are out. **Here is the point: successful people never quit, no matter how many times they have been beaten – a case in point is that of *Thomas Edison* – as long as they know exactly what path they are traveling and are convicted about it. As long as you thoughtfully stay the course and keep charting the waters, you will fail your way to success.**

13. Know what you came to get

Donald Trump said, "Success doesn't happen. It starts for those who take action." That means success and action must happen because action must take place before success is achieved. In fact, I say that to take action is to succeed. Nothing changes or comes about from inaction except what we never wanted in the first place. Network marketing is one industry that I know of that can take an ordinary person from nothing to an extraordinary change of lifestyle in a jiffy in comparison to what traditional business or and other types of earnings can yield, with very little risk.

14. Stick and stay until you get your pay. Stay the course to achieve.

Who is an achiever? An achiever is one who: (a) knows what he or she wants; (b) he or she takes action toward that, and (c) he or she stays the course to achieve. My finding is that most people are able to do 'a' and 'b' but never see the fruit of their labors because they do not stay long enough to see 'c' – staying the course to achieve. A lot of people quit easily. Some even think that to restructure and change course is a form of failure.

~In life and business, you don't get what you want or deserve, but what you negotiate and make happen!~

No, it is not. Rather, it is one of the essential ingredients for success. You must know when to restructure, regroup and reorganize and realign before going forward again after you have been through. Sometimes, it is necessary to go back in order to go forward successfully.

My advice: "stick and stay until you get your pay"

Stay in it long enough to flush out your losses and profit (this does not necessarily mean with the same company, products/services, but the idea of passive residual income opportunity that fits your need and objective).

15. Know when to dismount the dead horse (don't quit on your objective)

Experientially, from my very first network marketing test that I was in for almost four years, I learned the hard way that the first channel that you choose to get a taste of the residual income that comes from leveraging opportunities in network marketing may not be the one that takes you to the Promised Land. My husband and I left the company. Yet, we did not lose sight of earning a living using the power of leveraging and what it could do for our family if and when we got it right. So, we did not quit on our objective which is to find the right company, product and compensation plan that fits our lifestyle and still avail us the opportunity to earn walk-away residual income in a foreseeable future. However, that did not mean that we have given up on what we came for. It simply meant that that avenue was no longer fulfilling our needs. We decided to make the move when we found another promising company that proposed the right outline we had laid out for the criteria we made for which company to join. We found a match and right fit with PHPI, and so we are resting and earning restful increase instead of stressful increase. To God be the glory for the great things He has done.

16. The NUGGETS that seal the deal on whether you make it or not in this business

- It is a business and not a social network (that is, if that is your main objective for joining a network marketing business).

- Subdue or be subdued.

- Arrogate power to yourself – it belongs to nobody.

- Know when to bring your loved ones into the business, not necessarily when the overzealous and over-ambitious "up lines" tell you, so that you will not be a victim of no friends left **"NFL"**. Even if you have become a victim of NFL, it does not have to be fatal. Rather, it means that you have some repairing and restoring and explaining to do with them in time. Most people get over it with time and may be at a better place right now. So, give them the chance to say no. Just be honest with them, do not sugar coat anything and be sure to ask them this question: "What if it had worked out; would you be mad at me right now?" Be mindful that some will not come back and that is okay, because you don't need everyone to make it.

- Have and use integrity and honor in your business. Don't think that people are not watching even if they are not saying anything to you.

- Don't get into drama (it's not MMT).

- Don't NFL (No friends left) your life and net worth.

- Business is a war, but it is not worth your selling your soul.

- Get business partners.

- Work with positive and cooperative people.

- Develop a plan for ongoing communication.

- Motivate your team regularly.

- Be "you" and bring your uniqueness to the table.

- **Avoid network marketing "Junkies"; don't believe everything they tell you; investigate, but don't get caught in the paralysis of analysis.** That can be more dangerous than not investigating at all. I believe that it is better to take the chance and "fail" than not to try at all. I know for a fact that the worst chance to take is the one you did not take. Trust what we are sharing with you here for the simple reason that no one can preach or minister where they have not bled – if they do, you can see through them shortly thereafter. In addition to our many successful traditional businesses, I have been in the network business for about five years now and will stay with it for as long as it makes sense to do so.

- Avoid disgruntled and disloyal partners that are not team players (blackmailing and damaging the team which causes destruction and non-progressive advancements of the team). Conflict destroys concentration and production. Avoid it if you can!

Conclusion:

How do I conclude this book? Wow! I will not even attempt to conclude it with an opinion, because I did not write this book to convince anyone one way or the other. Rather I wrote it to share what I know about the industry and correct a few ill-conceived notions about the industry that are not true.

~In life and business, you don't get what you want or deserve, but what you <u>negotiate</u> and <u>make happen</u>!~

If you agree with me, you are right. If you disagree with me, you are also right. It is not about who is right and who is wrong. It is about each one doing what he/she believes will yield them the much-needed result of financial freedom. Oftentimes we fight for the wrong reasons – for why we believe what we believe and why we make the choices we make in life. I believe that the right fight should be goal- and result-oriented, because network marketing, particularly telecommunication, has given me a taste of what is possible with the concept of leveraging the talent and efforts of others and how it can change my family's generational wealth and well-being; I will fight for it for as long as I can.

Am I saying that by choosing PHPI as the company that has the right model and scheme to change many lives financially, that it is the only company that can? No! Not at all! I only used PHPI because it is the only company I've been able to find so far that fits my **"5-Tier Factorial Litmus Test"** that one must use when looking for the right company that can give one such an opportunity for a minimal investment, amongst other factors.

All you need to do instead of disagreeing or agreeing with my points here is to see what information, if any, that I have shared, speaks to you – even if it is just one word that you learned from the book – that could be the word that could help you bridge your current gap to get you to the next level in your life and business.

I also wanted to use this book to let people out there who have given up, because of one negative experience or another, on the idea of using network marketing as an avenue to earn a living, know that it **IS** a realistic way to start your own business and actually make good money from it. But you have to do some work in the beginning, and it is not magic like some would like or think. In spite of some bad people in the industry, you can learn how to avoid them and succeed if you *know how*, and I wanted to share some pointers and a few ideas of what has worked for me and many others who have succeeded in the industry.

I encourage you though, to not fight to hold onto the life you don't want or that you have been looking for new ways to improve upon, and use my journey and experiences and the success stories of others shared heretofore as your guide in network marketing or in life if you choose this path as a means of earning a living. In the end, is network marketing good for you and your business? You decide. All I did with this book is educate, empower, inform, create awareness and share in order to provoke your thoughts on the subject matter. To convince anyone to go one way or the other is definitely not one of my goals. Hopefully, in the end, it may make you do and earn differently than you have always known. Good luck!

To God be the Glory!

ORDER FORM

JAHS Publishing Group; www.jahspublishing.com

Name: _____

Company: _____

Address: _____

City/State: _____ Zip: _____

Telephone: _____ (Home) _____ (Work)

Fax: _____ E-mail: _____

Item	Price	No. Ordered	Total
Art, Poems & Stories of The Heart by Chi-Chi & Angel Dureke	$9.95	x _____	= _____
Words And Phrases of Wisdom by Margaret Dureke	$14.95	x _____	= _____
How To Succeed Against All Odds – Book, by Margaret Dureke	$14.95	x _____	= _____
How To Succeed Against All Odds - CD Audio Vol. I, by Margaret Dureke	$14.95	x _____	= _____
How To Succeed Against All Odds - CD Audio Vol. II, by Margaret Dureke	$14.95	x _____	= _____
Z-The Goodluck Bird by John Dureke, Jr.	$4.95	x _____	= _____

How to Succeed Against All Odds
by Margaret Dureke

Words & Phrases of Wisdom for
Spiritual & Emotional Upliftment
by Margaret Dureke

Eleven Proven Organizational & Time
Management Techniques
by Margaret Dureke

The Horrors Of War From The Eyes Of $8.95   x _____   = _____
A Child, by John Dureke, Jr.

7 Drivers For Success – (Circle Choice)
CD or Cassette, by Margaret Dureke $10.95   x _____   = _____

Subtotal $_____

Sales Tax
(Please add 5% for shipments to Maryland Residents)   _____

Shipping
($4.95 for first item and $1.50 for each additional item)   _____

Grand Total: $_____

Authorized Signature: _____ Date: _____

Please mail completed Order Form with a check or money order.
Order online at www.iahspublishing.com. For bulk orders, please email
info@iahspublishing.com or call: 301-864-2800.

COMING SOON! John Dureke's Cartoon Book Series.
(1) Memories of War; (2) Chi-Chi Rules Osha:
The cultural, fascinating, educational, entertaining
and funny stories for adults and children.

Made in the USA
Charleston, SC
17 October 2010